Projections of households
in England to 2021

1996-based estimates of the numbers

of households for regions

October 1999

Department of the Environment, Transport and the Regions: London

The Government Statistical Service

A service of statistical information and advice is provided to the Government by specialist staffs employed in the statistics divisions of individual Departments. Statistics are made generally available through their publication and further information and advice on them can be obtained from the Departments concerned.

Telephone queries about statistical series published in this volume should be addressed to the contact points listed on the contents page opposite. Written queries should be addressed to:

Housing Data and Statistics Division
Department of the Environment
Floor 1/H3 Eland House
Bressenden Place
London SW1E 5DU

Department of the Environment, Transport and the Regions
Eland House
Bressenden Place
London SW1E 5DU
Telephone 0171 890 3000
Internet service http://www.detr.gov.uk/

Further copies of this report are available from:

Department of the Environment, Transport and the Regions
Publications Sale Centre
Unit 21
Goldthorpe Industrial Estate
Goldthorpe
Rotherham S63 9BL
Tel: 01709 891318
Fax: 01709 881673

ISBN 1 85112 326 1

Printed in Great Britain on material containing 75% post-consumer waste and 25% ECF pulp (cover); 100% post-consumer waste (text). C9100 October 1999

CONTENTS

Executive Summary

INTRODUCTION

This publication sets out the new (1996-based) projections of the numbers of households by Government Office Regions to the year 2021. They are based on recent trends in household formation, official projections of the population in each area and official projections of marital status. They supersede the 1992-based projections published in 1995. Analyses are presented for the first time that illustrate the effects on the projections of changes in key parameters.

These official projections are trend based. They illustrate what would happen if past trends in household formation were to continue into the future. The projections are heavily dependent on the demographic assumptions used, particularly international and internal migration, the marital status projections and the continuation of past trends in household formation. They are not policy-based forecasts of what the Government expects or intends to happen.

NATIONAL HOUSEHOLD PROJECTIONS

The number of households in England is projected to grow from 20.2 million in 1996 to 24.0 million by 2021, an increase of 3.8 million, or 19%. The biggest increase is in the number of one person households which is projected to grow by 2.7 million, from 5.8 million in 1996 to 8.5 million by 2021, 71% of the total increase in the number of households.

Cohabiting couple households are projected to grow by 1.3 million from 1.5 million to 2.8 million, an increase partially offset by the continued decline in married couple households from 10.2 million to 9.2 million. Taking married and cohabiting couples together, couple households are expected to grow by 0.2 million. Lone parent households are projected to grow by 0.1 million and other multi-person households by 0.7 million.

The average size of household, which dropped from 2.86 people in 1971 to 2.40 people in 1996, is projected to continue to fall, and reach 2.15 people per household by 2021.

Slightly more than three quarters of the projected increase in the number of households can be attributed to changes in the size and age structure of the adult population.

SENSITIVITY ANALYSIS

The Government accepted the recommendations of the 1998 Environment Select Committee Inquiry on Housing that household projections should be accompanied by measures of their sensitivities to changes in key parameters. It was only possible to carry out this analysis at national level with the data currently available. The analysis shows, for example, that if international migration increased or decreased by 40 thousand per annum over the projection period, this could mean a projected change at national level at 2021 of over 0.4 million households. Similarly, if real interest rates throughout the period were 1 percentage point higher or lower, the projected number of households in 2021 could change by over 0.2 million.

REGIONAL HOUSEHOLD PROJECTIONS

Although the numbers of households in all regions are projected to increase over the period 1996 to 2021, the size of the increases varies across England. The South East, East of England and the South West are all projected to have around a quarter more households in 2021 than in 1996. For London and East Midlands growth is around a fifth and in other areas projected growth is significantly lower. The North East has the lowest projected growth of just 8%.

COMPARISONS WITH PREVIOUS HOUSEHOLD PROJECTIONS

The previous 1992-based household projections, published in 1995, showed an increase of 4.4 million households between 1991 and 2016. The 1996-based projections, published here, show an increase of 4.1 million over the same period. There are a number of reasons for the change in the projected number of households. Nationally the population at 2016 is projected to be higher which would, all other things being equal, result in an increase of over 0.1 million households. However this increase has been more than offset by a fall of around 0.4 million households due to changes in the marital status projections. These changes are complex. Increases projected in the overall numbers of married and cohabiting couples are not matched by a corresponding reduction in the number of younger adults living alone. There is a projected fall in one person households of over 0.6 million at 2016 compared with the 1992-based projections. This is made up of large falls in older age groups combined with a small rise in the younger age groups. At 2016 there is a fall of over 0.5 million in those aged 65 or over living alone, a fall of over 0.2 million in those between 45 and 64 living alone, but a rise of around 0.1 million in the number of people under 45 living alone. In particular, there is a projected fall of 0.4 million formerly married women aged 65 and over living alone.

Introduction

Estimates of the number of households in future years are required for a number of purposes, at national, regional and more local levels. In *Planning for the Communities of the Future* (Cm 3885, 1998) the Government stated (paragraph 26) that the Department of the Environment, Transport and the Regions (DETR) would continue to use the official national population projections for producing household projections. The 1996-based national population projections were prepared in 1997 by the Government Actuary's Department in consultation with the Registrars General. The Office for National Statistics (ONS) published new 1996-based subnational population projections in 1998. These projections of the population are the basis for the 1996-based household projections published in this volume. They are the most recent in a series that began with the projections published by the Ministry of Housing and Local Government in 1969 and supersede the 1992-based projections published in 1995.

This publication presents projections of households in England in total, Government Office and standard statistical regions up to 2021. Comparisons with the previous projections are presented at regional as well as national level. Local government reorganisation including boundary changes, which have taken place since the 1992-based projections, have not materially affected the boundaries of Government Office and standard statistical regions.

The household projections are trend based, in the sense that they illustrate how many households would form from the projected future population if past trends in household formation were to continue into the future. They are, therefore, not policy based forecasts of what the Government expects to happen or intends to happen, either nationally or subnationally. However a continuation of past trends does provide a starting point for assessing future prospects, especially when the trends appear firmly established over an extended period. Examples are the increasing proportion of widows and widowers who live independently and more recently, the proportion of middle aged men and women who live alone rather than in couples.

The household projections are dependent on the population projections from which they are derived. Table 4 shows that of the total projected net increase in households in the projection period from 1996 to 2021, three quarters is the result of the growth of the total adult population and changes in its age structure. In view of its importance for the projection of households, the population projection is discussed in some detail (in Annex C). The official national population projections are prepared by the Government Actuary's Department, on assumptions agreed between interested Government Departments and are used for many official policy purposes, of which estimates of the number of households in the future years are but one. Assumptions about future births, which affect the number of households only towards the end of the projection period, deaths and migration are part of the projections of population. The subnational population projections form an important assumption for the distribution of future households. These are not discussed here as the analyses reported concentrate on the national household projection. However, changes were made to the methodology underlying the 1996-based subnational population projections, see PP3 No 10 (1999) for further details.

Since the contribution of the population projections to the projected increases in households is large, indications are given of how sensitive the household projections are to small differences in the demographic assumptions - births, deaths, migration, marriage and divorce rates and cohabitation. In its reply to the House of Commons Environment Committee (Cm 4080, 1998, paragraphs 124 and 125), the Government stated its acceptance of the Committee's recommendation that indications should be given of the sensitivity of the household projections to small differences in key assumptions.

Uncertainties in demographic projections, including the number of households that will form from a population of given size, age structure, marital status and proportion cohabiting, increase with distance into the future. Uncertainties increase also with the degree of detail, both by categories of household and geographically. That uncertainty increases with geographical detail is an important constraint on the local government areas for which robust projections of households can be made. The smaller the population, the greater, generally speaking, is the difference between a projection and a forecast. But for all projection figures the caveat applies that figures shown to the nearest thousand, to avoid problems of rounding, do not purport to be as precise as that.

The methodology and definitions for the household projections are the same as used in the 1992-based projections; the only significant change has been to introduce data from the Labour Force Survey (discussed in Annex B) to bring to account changes in household formation after 1992. The description in the report on the 1992-based projections (DoE (1995)) of the changes in definitions and methodology are therefore not repeated here.

Unchanged from the 1992-based projections and from all sets of household projections back to 1981 are the concept and definition of a household. The definition (see Annex A) is wholly separate from that of a dwelling. A household can live in only part of a dwelling, as considerable numbers still do. In times past, much larger numbers of households occupied only part of a dwelling, either because they could not afford the rent of self contained accommodation (as at the time of the 1911 Census, for instance) or because of housing shortage (as in 1945 and the two following decades). The projections of future numbers of households are therefore not projections of dwellings.

The main change from the presentation of the previous (1992-based) projections has been to include measures of sensitivity to changes in assumptions about future births, deaths, migration, marriages, divorces and cohabitation. An attempt has also been made to provide an indication of the sensitivity of the future rate of increase in households to economic conditions in the medium to long term. The variables examined were real income per head, real interest rates and unemployment. These variables have a bearing on the number of people who can afford to live independently. The scope for economic assumptions to influence future increases in the number of households is constrained by the high proportion of the projected increase that results from the growth of the adult population and changes in its age structure.

This publications has three parts:

(a) an explanatory commentary, of the main household totals (analysed by type of household) in the 1996-based projections at national level, including comparisons with the 1992-based projections and a brief summary of the regional household totals;

(b) detailed national tables and less detailed tables for regions; and

(c) a series of annexes with details of definitions; methodology and data sources; the 1996-based national projections of population, marital status and cohabitation; the institutional population; comparison with the 1992-based projections and earlier projections; and sensitivity to changes in demographic assumptions and future economic conditions.

The household projection model was developed over a number of years by the late Dr Ian Corner at the Building Research Establishment. These projections would not have been possible but for his hard work and expertise in developing this model. These projections would also not have been possible without the work of Professor David King and his team at Anglia Polytechnic University and Dr Alan Holmans, Cambridge University who carried the projections work forward after the untimely death of Dr Corner.

Results and comparisons with 1992-based projections

1. National household totals

Table 1 shows the projected total of households, analysed by type of household, at five year intervals between 1996 (the base year) and 2021, with estimates for 1971, 1981 and 1991 shown for comparison. The figures for 1996 were derived in the same way as those for 2001 and beyond, by using the projection model as described in Annex B. A direct estimate of the number of households in 1996, outside the projection model, may be made by combining the grossed totals from the Survey of English Housing for 1995/96, 1996/97 and 1997/98 (ONS 1997, 1998 and 1999). This gives 20.160 million. That is sufficiently close to the projection of 20.186 million for 1996 in Table 1 for that figure to be treated as the estimated actual total.

Over the 25 years from 1996 to 2021, the number of separate households in England is projected to increase by 3.81 million. This is a smaller increase than actually occurred in the previous quarter century from 1971 to 1996, when the number of households is estimated to have increased by 4.24 million. Of the projected increase of 3.81 million households, 71% or 2.70 million, are one person households. The number of one person households is estimated to have increased by 2.85 million between 1971 and 1996, 67% of the estimated total increase in the number of households in that period. The projected change between 1996 and 2021 is compared with the past change between 1971 and 1996 for each type of household in Table 6 below and discussed in section 3.

It is estimated that married couple households formed 71% of all households in 1971. This percentage decreased to just over 50% in 1996 and is projected to fall still further to 38% in 2021. The increase in cohabitation over the two periods has not and will not fully compensate for these decreases. The number of married couple households and cohabiting couple households together fell as a percentage of all households from an estimated 72% in 1971 to 58% in 1996 and is projected to decrease further to just under 50% in 2021. On the other hand the number of one person households as a percentage of all households increased from 19% in 1971 to 29% in 1996 and is projected to increase further to just over 35% in 2021.

Average household size, not to be confused with "the size of the average family", is projected to fall by 0.25 persons, from 2.40 to 2.15 persons per household, between 1996 and 2021, distinctly less than the 0.46 persons reduction in the previous quarter century. Further back in time, the fall in average household size was more rapid, equivalent to 0.61 per quarter century between 1911 and 1971. The increase in the proportion of one person households that has occurred, and is projected to continue, reduces the average numbers of persons per household and explains about 40 per cent of the reduction in average household size both between 1971 to 1996 and between 1996 to 2021. Between 1911 and 1971, the proportion was only 20 per cent, as decreasing family size had a larger impact on the reduction in average household size in this period.

The household types in Table 1 are defined in Annex A. Concealed couples and concealed lone parent families are also shown. Their numbers are small, in part as a consequence of the rules for selecting the household representative. To be identified as concealed, a couple has to live in same household as another couple. If a couple is present in a household the household is automatically classified as a couple household.

In Table 1, as in subsequent tables in this report, figures are shown to the nearest thousand for arithmetical reasons, to permit proportions and differences to be calculated more accurately than would be possible with more heavily rounded figures. As mentioned in the Introduction, presenting the projection results in this detail does not imply that they are considered to be accurate to the nearest thousand. In the tables the detail does not always add to the totals owing to rounding.

Table 1	Summary of Household Estimates and Projections 1971 - 2021: England									
	Household (thousands)						Concealed Families (thousands)		Average household size	
	Married couple	Cohabiting couple	Lone parent	Other multi-person	One person	Total	Couple	Lone Parent	All h'holds	Multi-person h'holds
1971	11,249	204	381	1,165	2,953	15,951	126	105	2.86	3.28
1981 (a)	11,013	500	625	1,234	3,934	17,306	83	82	2.67	3.16
1991 (b)	10,552	1 177	974	1,007	5,142	19,213	74	91	2.47	3.01
1996	10,190	1,479	1,168	1,543	5,806	20,186	63	89	2.40	2.96
2001	9,829	1,896	1,258	1,676	6,333	20,992	59	87	2.34	2.92
2006	9,535	2,251	1,293	1,836	6,819	21,733	59	89	2.29	2.88
2011	9,357	2,509	1,299	2,012	7,342	22,519	63	90	2.24	2.84
2016	9,251	2,660	1,296	2,172	7,934	23,313	67	89	2.19	2.81
2021	9,157	2,761	1,288	2,286	8,509	24,000	72	88	2.15	2.79

Notes:(a) Revised estimate hence differs from Table I of *Projections of Households in England to 2016*

(b) Differs from Table I of *Projections of Households in England to 2016* owing to revisions to the estimates of legal marital status (see *Population Trends No 89*) and cohabitation

Population growth, especially in the adult population, is a fundamental cause of increases in the number of households. The adult population does not necessarily grow at the same rate as the total population. The projected increase in households between 1996 and 2021 is shown in Table 2 along with the increase in total population and in the population aged 20 and over. To provide a longer term perspective, a comparison is made not only with 1971-1996 as in Table 1, but back to 1901 as well. Figures for England and Wales have been used up until 1971, and figures for England alone from 1971.

Table 2 shows that the adult population grew more quickly before 1951 than it has since, averaged over a number of years. In addition, the growth in the number of households in percentage terms, is slowing down.

Table 2	Long Term Comparison of Population and Households		
	Households	**Total population**	**Population aged 20 and over**
In thousands			
1901 (a)	7,007	32,528	18,736
1911 (a)	8,005	36,070	21,653
	7,943		
1931	10,233	39,952	26,988
1951 (b)	13,259	43,758	31,362
1971	16,709	49,152	34,152
	15,951	46,412	32,246
1996	20,186	49,089	36,740
2021	24,000	52,483	40,767
Annual average rates of increase (per cent a year)			
1901 - 31	1.3	0.7	1.2
1931 - 51	1.3	0.5	0.8
1951 - 71	1.2	0.6	0.4
1971 - 96	0.9	0.2	0.5
1996 - 2021	0.7	0.3	0.4

Notes (a)"Separate occupiers" in 1901 and 1911 not exactly comparable with "private families" and "households".

(b) Includes estimated number of households in Services family quarters etc. not enumerated separately

Source: Population and households in England and Wales 1901 to 1971, see DoE(1977) table I.2 and I.5, *National Population Projections 1996-based*, PP2 No 21 (1999), for population data for 1996 and 2021.

Increases in households and population may also be compared in absolute terms because, as in Table 2, the base from which they are calculated influences percentage rates of change. The increases over the 25 year projection period, 1996 to 2021, need to be compared with equally long periods. This can be done exactly with 1971 - 96. Before then twenty or thirty year periods have to be taken, see Table 3.

Table 3	Long Period Increases in Population and Households (thousands)			
	Increase in total population	**Increase in population aged 20 and over**	**Increase in households**	**Annual average increase in households**
1901 - 1931	7,424	8,252	3,288	110
1931 – 1951 (a)	3,806	4,374	3,026	151
1951 – 1971 (a)	5,394	2,790	3,450	173
1971 - 1996	2,677	4,494	4,235	169
1996 - 2021	3,394	4,027	3,814	153

Note: (a) The increase in households between 1931 and 1951 was held down and between 1951 and 1971 enhanced, by the very large number of couples living as "concealed families" in 1951.

The adult population grew by more than the total population, with the exception of 1951 - 71. The faster growth of the total population than that of the adult population between 1951 and 1971 is explained by the so-called baby boom between the mid 1950s and mid 1960s. A faster rise in the adult population than in the total population is an important reason why the number of households can rise faster than the total population, though not the only one. A faster increase in the adult population than in the total population is in prospect in the quarter century to 2021. But even the total population is far from static and is projected to increase by some 135,000 a year. The projected rise in the household forming population is faster, at 160,000 a year. The projected annual increase in households between 1996 and 2021 is 153,000, 16,000 a year less than in the previous quarter century, 20,000 less than in 1951-71 and only fractionally more than in 1931-51.

2. Components of the increase in the total of households

Splitting the increase in household numbers into four component parts can show the relationship between the increase in the number of households and the increase in the population more clearly. The components are:

(a) the projected growth of the total adult private household population;

(b) the change in the age structure of the population;

(c) changes in the marital status of the population, including proportions cohabiting, as well as legal marital status; and

(d) changes in household representative rates specific for age, sex, legal marital status and cohabitation. Household representative rates are defined in Annex A.

An analysis of the projected net increase in households divided into these four components, together with a similar analysis of the net increase in households between 1971 and 1996 for comparison, is shown in Table 4. The table includes a "remainder" column, which shows the change due to interaction between the components, for instance, increases in household representative rates applied to the increase in the adult population.

Table 4	Components of the Past and Projected Increase in Households 1971 - 2021: England				
	Adult population	Age structure	Marital status (a)	Household representative rates	Remainder	Total
1971 - 81	912	-86	-192	636	85	1,356
1981 - 91	803	498	-167	624	149	1,906
1991 - 96	281	428	-146	334	65	973
1996 - 2001	413	166	-76	279	24	806
2001 - 06	519	2	-16	229	8	741
2006 - 11	485	116	3	176	6	786
2011 - 16	419	233	8	132	3	794
2016 - 21	326	264	-1	99	-	687
1971 - 96	1,996	841	-506	1,605	299	4,235
1996 - 2021	2,163	780	-84	914	40	3,814

Note (a) Includes proportions cohabiting

The increase in the adult population arithmetically explains some 57 per cent of the projected net increase in the number of households between 1996 and 2021, compared with 47 per cent in the previous quarter century. The changing age structure accounts for a further 20 per cent in both twenty five year periods. Changes in the size of the adult population and its age structure thus explain 67 per cent of the estimated increase in the number of households in the quarter century from 1971 to 1996 and 77 per cent of the projected increase between 1996 and 2021. Thus the national population projection can be seen to make a very powerful contribution to the projected increase in households. It is therefore described in some detail in Annex C, where the effects of net inward migration and falling morality are presented in quantitative terms. Because the time periods shown in Table 4 are not of equal length, a version in terms of annual averages is shown in Table 5.

Table 5	Components of Past and Projected Change in Households in Terms of Annual Averages			
	Adult population total and age structure	Household representative rates	Other	Total
1971 - 81	83	64	-11	136
1981 - 91	130	62	-2	191
1991 - 96	142	69	-16	195
1996 - 2001	116	56	-10	161
2001 - 06	104	46	-2	148
2006 - 11	120	35	2	157
2011 - 16	130	26	2	159
2016 - 21	118	20	-3	137

Table 5 shows that the contribution of past changes in the adult population and its age structure to the increase in the number of separate households have been much more variable than the changes in household representative rates. That the population effect was much larger in 1981 - 91 and 1991 - 96 than in 1971 - 81 was the result of the "baby boom" birth cohorts (from 1956 to the end of the 1960s) reaching adulthood. The contribution of population change to the projected increase in households runs lower in the 1996 - 2006 decade because the fall in births in the later 1960s and in the first half of the 1970s will reduce the number reaching adulthood in those years. However, much of the lagged effect of this fall in births is offset by net inward migration.

The increase in the number of households due to rising household representative rates was very similar in 1981-91 to what it had been in 1971-81, even though the increase in households due to population change was different. This is important evidence for the increase in household representative rates being largely autonomous with respect to population change, as the projection model (see Annex B) assumes. If the effect of population change and household representative rates on the increase in households were jointly determined, the increase in household representative rates would be higher when the effect of population change was lower and vice versa. This was not what happened in 1971-81 and 1981-91, nor in 1991-96.

The contribution of rising household representative rates to the increase in the number of households is projected to diminish with time. The main reason is that in more and more population categories, household representative rates will be approaching 100 per cent. As they approach that level, by definition the maximum, the rise must necessarily slow down. For this reason, the projected net increase in households in the last five year period of the projection period due to rising household representative rates is barely more than a third of what is projected in the first five year period. The same point may be put another way by noting that in 1996-2001, 36 per cent of the projected increase in households is due to rising household representative rates, but only 14 per cent in 2016-2021.

3. Types of household

Both in 1971 to 1996 and in the projection period from 1996 to 2021, the numbers of households in the five categories of household types changed in very different ways. These household types are defined in Annex A and also the relationships between marital status and type of household. Analyses are made of the different types by age and, where relevant, sex and marital status. To set the scene, Table 6 shows projected net changes in the number of household representatives of each type in total, with corresponding changes in 1971-96. The first part of the table gives the total household growth for the periods. The second part of the table shows the changes in the number of concealed families, the number of wives and cohabiting female partners in couple households and adults (20 and over) who are not household representatives or wives or cohabiting partners. The sum of the household representatives and the other representatives gives the total private household population aged 20 and over.

Table 6	Actual Changes in Number of Households by Type for 1971 - 96 and Projected for 1996 - 2021 (thousands)	
Household representatives	**1971 - 96**	**1996 - 2021**
Married couple household representatives	-1,059	-1,033
Cohabiting couple household representatives	+1,275	+1,282
(All couple household representatives)	(+216)	(+249)
Lone parent household representatives	+787	+120
Other multi-person household representatives	+378	+743
One person household representatives	+2,853	+2,703
All household representatives	**+4,235**	**+3,814**
Concealed couple representatives	-63	+9
Concealed lone parent family representatives	-16	-1
Wives and female partners in couples	+153	+258
Other adults (20 and over)	+156	-43
Private household population aged 20 and over	**+4,467**	**+3,994**

Note: The individual categories do not sum exactly to the change in the private household population aged 20 and over because of the small numbers of household representatives aged 15-19.

Both in 1971-96 and in the projection period, the reduction in married couple households is slightly more than offset by an increase in cohabiting couples. In a subsequent section the way in which the changing balance between married and cohabiting couples is related to age is discussed. Also examined is how much of the increase in cohabitation is by never married men and women and the changing proportions of men and women living in couples.

For lone parent households, in contrast to the other types of household, the projected increase from 1996-2021 is much smaller than the actual increase in 1971-96. Here the distinction between legally never married lone parents and those divorced and separated is extremely important and is discussed in more detail below. The falling number of married couples, particularly at the ages where the incidence of separation and divorce is highest, must necessarily constrain the number of divorced lone parents.

Other multi-person households are a heterogeneous group. The household projection model does not distinguish the different groupings within the category, such as lone parents with only non-dependent children. But an analysis by age and marital status provides some pointers, along with survey information (from the Labour Force Survey) about the composition of these households.

One person households amounted to 67 per cent of the total net increase in households between 1971 and 1996 and to 71 per cent in the projection period from 1996 to 2021. They are a very heterogeneous category as well as being very large and therefore require discussion in some detail. Moreover, the changes in their number according to the 1996-based projections are different in important ways from the 1992-based projection (see below and in more detail in Annex F).

3A COUPLE HOUSEHOLDS

The aggregate comparisons of the change in the number of married couples and cohabiting couples in Tables 1 and 6 may be disaggregated by age. In 1971 cohabitation was uncommon in comparison with marriage; by 1996 cohabiting couples had become much more numerous and in the projection period a large further increase in cohabiting couples is expected. The early growth in cohabitation was among younger men and women. Between 1971 and 1981 the number of cohabiting couples increased by just under 300,000; 210,000 of the additional male partners and 225,000 of the female partners were under aged 35. Table 7 shows how the change in the balance between married and cohabiting couples has changed, and is projected to change, at successively higher ages.

Table 7	Married and Cohabiting Couples Analysed by Age (thousands)							
	Age of Husband or Male Partner							
	Under 25	25-29	30-34	35-44	45-54	55-64	65 and over	Total
1971								
Married	648	1,093	1,131	2,287	2,369	2,177	1,671	11,375
Cohabiting	24	26	24	43	39	30	19	205
1981								
Married	418	942	1,312	2,287	2,129	2,028	1,978	11,095
Cohabiting	96	104	85	105	57	34	20	501
1996								
Married	88	557	1,029	2,217	2,335	1,841	2,172	10,239
Cohabiting	214	388	311	324	174	53	29	1,493
2006								
Married	56	267	569	2,099	2,135	2,147	2,296	9,569
Cohabiting	260	389	393	671	336	162	65	2,276
2021								
Married	55	291	565	1,410	1,830	2,196	2,839	9,187
Cohabiting	267	441	450	658	529	328	130	2,802

Note: The concealed couples shown in Table 1 are included here, hence the differences from the number of households given in Tables 1 and 5

In 1996, cohabiting couples far outnumbered married couples in the under 25 year age group. By 2006, cohabiting couples are projected to outnumber married couples at ages 25-29. By 2021 they will be starting to approach the number of married couples in the 30-34 age range. The increase of some 1.3 million cohabiting couples between 1971 and 1996 was divided between never legally married and formerly married male partners in proportions approximately 70:30. But nearly all of the projected net increase in cohabiting couples between 1996 and 2021 are couples with legally never married male partners. The reason for the contrast is that, after a pause at the beginning of the 1990s, the rising trend in the proportion of legally never married men and women cohabiting resumed and is projected to continue (see Annex D), whereas the proportion of divorced men and women cohabiting has levelled off, after rising during the 1980s. In addition, falling marriage rates will work through to falling numbers of divorces and a smaller divorced population.

A question of some importance is how the actual changes in the number of married and cohabiting couples shown in Table 7 reflect changes in the proportion of people living in couples as distinct from alone or in someone else's household. This is discussed in Annex D. Table D.7 shows that falling marriage rates have been only partly offset by more cohabitation and the number of couple households has been further reduced by divorce. There has been a reduction in the proportion of men and women at the young and middle ages who live in couples, and this trend is projected to continue. This is one of the principal reasons for the projected increase in the number of men and women living alone as one person households.

First marriage rates in the 40 and over age groups have long been low; the falling proportion of middle aged and older men who are married is the consequence of past falls in marriage rates. Similarly, the rising proportion of middle aged and older men who are cohabiting is primarily the consequence of men who began to cohabit when young continuing to cohabit as they age. Whether that is with the same partners is not known: there is very little information about the dynamics of cohabitation in the longer term.

The effect of more or fewer men and women cohabiting is discussed later under the heading of variant projections, in summary form later in this part of the report and more fully in Annex G. The effect is complex. The effect on the number of households would not be a net reduction of one household for each additional cohabiting couple; even ignoring those couples who cohabit instead of getting married. This is because not all non-married non-cohabiting men and women at the ages where cohabitation is most prevalent live independently. The projected net reduction in the total number of separate households as a result of more cohabiting is equal to about one third of the additional cohabiting couples, if there is no reduction in the number of married couples.

3B LONE PARENT HOUSEHOLDS

Most lone parent households are lone mother households. Never married lone father households are very few, some 11,000 in 1996. Formerly married (divorced, separated or widowed) lone father households numbered 117,000; never married lone mother households were 400,000 and formerly married lone mother households 640,000. The distinction in practical terms between never legally married and formerly married lone parents is, however, becoming increasingly blurred through the increase in the number of cohabiting couples with children. Both parents at the same address (Population Trends No 94 Table 10) registered the births of nearly 60 per cent of all children born outside marriage. Such parents are almost certainly cohabiting. In 1997 such births in England and Wales numbered 142,000 compared with 404,000 births within marriage. Whether separation rates for cohabiting couples with children exceed divorce rates in the same way as separation rates for all cohabiting couples is not known. But clearly there are enough cohabiting couples with children for a significant number of never married lone mothers to have had their children while cohabiting. Support for this inference is reported in J. Haskey "One Parent Families and Their Dependent Children", *Population Trends* No 94, who cited findings from the ONS Omnibus Survey, though only for a small sample of never married lone mothers.

The distinction between never married lone mothers who bore their children while members of a cohabiting couple household and other never married lone mothers cannot be drawn in the 1996-based household projections or in the corresponding figures for earlier years. The analysis has therefore to be in terms of never (legally) married and formerly married (including legally married but with no usually resident spouse). Table 8 compares the projected figures between 1996 and 2021 with the corresponding figures for 1971, 1981 and 1991. There are too few lone father households to draw a similar distinction. Concealed lone parent families are also shown.

Table 8	Lone Parent Households and Families (thousands)					
	Lone parent households	Concealed lone parent families	Total lone parent families	Male lone parents	Formerly married female lone parents	Never married female lone parents
1971	381	105	486	75	330	80
1981	625	82	708	119	456	133
1991	975	91	1,066	115	601	350
1996	1,168	89	1,257	142	656	458
2001	1,258	87	1,345	152	650	543
2006	1,293	89	1,381	154	611	617
2011	1,299	90	1,389	146	558	685
2016	1,296	89	1,386	138	512	736
2021	1,288	88	1,376	131	486	759

The projected halt to the increase and then the fall in the number of lone parent families is shown to be the result of a fall after 2001 in the number of formerly married lone parents (including men) and slowing of the increase of never married female lone parents. The reason for the fall in the number of formerly married lone parents is that the prolonged fall in marriage rates has reduced, and will continue to reduce, the number of married men and women who might potentially separate and divorce at ages when their children are still dependent. In other words, the projected fall in the number of formerly married lone mothers (and fathers) is a delayed action consequence of the fall in the number of younger married couples. Lower mortality at the ages of parents with dependent children has resulted in widows becoming a smaller and smaller proportion of lone parents. In 1971, there were an estimated 100,000 widows and 27,000 widowers who were lone parents, but in 2021 there are projected to be 23,000 widows and 12,000 widower lone parents. In 1971, 26 per cent of lone parent families had widowed heads, in 1996, 5 per cent, and in 2021 the projected proportion is just under 3 per cent.

After rising by over 20,000 a year between 1981 and 1991, and only just under 20,000 a year between 1991 and 1996, the number of never married lone mothers is projected to rise by 17,000 a year between 1996 to 2001, and then by 15,000, 14,000, 10,000 and 5,000 for each subsequent five year period. The changing age structure of the female population is important for the slowing of the increase in the number of never married lone mother families. Most lone parents are under age 40 (94 per cent of never married lone mothers in 1996), and a high proportion under 35 (84 per cent). This is because the definition of a dependent child is one under 16 or 16 - 18 if in full time education. A lone parent living with an older son or daughter would be classified as a multi-person household. The female population aged 20 - 39 rose by nearly 600,000 between 1981 and 1991; there was a further small increase between 1991 and 1996 and then the population projection indicates a fall of between 750,000 and 800,000 in the three five year periods from 1996 to 2011. The rising trend in the number of never married mothers under aged 20 with dependent children is projected into the future, to reach 49,000 in 2021 compared with 34,000 in 1996. The increase in their number in the projection period (15,000) is equal to 5 per cent of the total projected increase in never married lone mother families.

3C OTHER MULTI-PERSON HOUSEHOLDS

These form a residual category, defined by exception as multi-person households that are neither married couple, nor cohabiting couple, nor lone parent households. Lone parents with only non-dependent children come into this category, as do brothers and sisters and more distant relations (excluding grand parents and dependent grand children - see Annex A). Also included are households of two or more unrelated adults, for instance flat sharers. The household projection procedure does not distinguish sub-categories and its data set does not include any information about other household members or their relationship to the household representative. The projected increase in the number of this household type (see Table 1) is sufficiently large to warrant an attempt to see what can be inferred from the information about the household representatives, namely age, marital status and sex. Lone parents with only non-dependent children, for example, are likely to be female, formerly married and over 45. As a starting point, Table 9 analyses representatives of other multi-person households in 1996 by sex, marital status and broad age ranges.

Table 9	Other Multi-Person Households in 1996: Analysis by Sex, Marital Status and Age (thousands)				
	Male		**Female**		**Total**
Age	Never married	Formerly married	Never married	Formerly married	
Under 30	184	10	49	2	245
30 - 44	120	93	43	72	329
45 - 64	49	172	22	317	560
65 and over	38	108	25	237	409
Total	**392**	**384**	**139**	**628**	**1,543**

Changes between 1971 and 1996 and between 1996 and 2021 are given in Table 10.

In all "other multi-person households" containing both men and women, except those with a lone parent with non-dependent children, the oldest male member is the household representative (see Annex A). The household would be classified according to his age and marital status. In a household containing a lone parent with only non-dependent children, the parent is the household representative. In official surveys such as the Labour Force Survey (LFS) which by reason of its sample size is used here as the source of information about the composition of the "other multi-person households", the criteria for selecting the household head are different. The household head is the person in whose name the accommodation is owned or rented; if it is jointly owned or rented, then the household head is the oldest male joint owner or tenant; or if all the joint owners or tenants are female, the eldest. That limits the comparability of the survey data with the household projection figures. The survey data (from LFS for 1996/97) are nevertheless enlightening. They show that high proportions of "other multi-person households" headed by formerly married men and women aged 45-64 and 65 and over are lone parents with only non-dependent children. For formerly married men aged 45-64 and 65 and over the proportions shown by 1996/97 LFS are 45 per cent and 59 per cent and for formerly married women of these ages 83 per cent and 66 per cent respectively. The "other multi-person households" with never married heads - who are for the most part under age 45 - are a more varied mix of household types. Male and female heads under age 45 are taken together, owing to the difference between the way the rules work for selecting the household representative in household projections and the household head in housing surveys. Then 27 per cent of these households comprised two unrelated adults of the same sex; 7 per cent comprised two adults of opposite sex; 10 per cent were households of three adults all of the same sex, and 7 per cent were three adult households, not all of the same sex. 9 per cent consisted of two related adults. All the above were households with no dependent children. Another 21 per cent were other types of household without dependent children. Also included were some households classified as lone parents with only non-dependent children, some 17 per cent of "other multi-person households" with never married heads aged under 45.

Table 10 Estimated and Projected Changes in "Other Multi-Person Households" Between 1971 and 1996 and Between 1996 and 2021 (thousands)		
Sex, Marital Status and Age of the Household Representative	1971 to 1996	1996 to 2021
Never married male		
Under 30	+142	+56
30 - 44	+91	+78
45 - 64	-33	+38
65 and over	-11	-10
Total	**+189**	**+161**
Formerly married male		
Under 30	+4	-4
30 - 44	+71	-32
45 - 64	+91	+131
65 and over	-5	+103
Total	**+162**	**+198**
Never married female		
Under 30	+26	+12
30 - 44	+31	+43
45 - 64	-13	+46
65 and over	-57	-16
Total	**-14**	**+85**
Formerly married female		
Under 30	+1	-1
30 - 44	+57	-14
45 - 64	+103	+242
65 and over	-121	+73
Total	**+40**	**+300**
All other multi-person households	**+378**	**+743**

A projected increase in the quarter century to 2021 of some 370,000 households of lone parents with only non-dependent children, one third males and two thirds females, results from applying survey based proportions of lone parents with only non-dependent children to the projected increases in "other multi-person households" with formerly married representatives aged 45-64 and 65 and over. These increases in lone parent households with only non-dependent children are the counterpart of the falling number of lone parent households with dependent children shown in Table 8. The number of formerly married lone parents with dependent children is projected to fall by some 185,000 between 1996 and 2021, but the number of lone parent households with only non-dependent children is likely to rise by 180,000 more than this. With the passage of time the children of lone parents cease to be dependent in the technical sense and the households to which they belong change from lone parent to "other multi-person households". The much greater variety among "other multi-person households" with representatives who are never married and under age 45 precludes anything as specific being said about what is implied by the projected increases of 135,000 with male and 55,000 with female representatives. But an increase in the number of "flat share" type households would seem implied.

3D ONE PERSON HOUSEHOLDS

Table 11 One Person Households: Analysis by Marital Status and Age (thousands)			
	1971	**1996**	**2021**
Never married male			
Under 30	95	407	521
30 - 34	27	249	364
35 - 44	55	231	601
45 - 54	68	135	521
55 - 64	72	101	366
65 - 74	43	93	160
75 and over	14	46	76
Total	**374**	**1,260**	**2,607**
Formerly married male			
Under 30	17	30	19
30 - 34	15	72	41
35 - 44	33	198	150
45 - 54	50	228	285
55 - 64	98	184	406
65 - 74	139	224	391
75 and over	119	291	465
Total	**469**	**1,226**	**1,755**
Never married female			
Under 30	60	245	310
30 - 34	15	126	177
35 - 44	36	124	322
45 - 54	66	75	322
55 - 64	127	68	214
65 - 74	151	92	97
75 and over	102	119	73
Total	**559**	**851**	**1,513**
Formerly married female			
Under 30	10	21	11
30 - 34	6	34	21
35 - 44	20	96	72
45 - 54	87	187	171
55 - 64	328	325	394
65 - 74	595	685	712
75 and over	497	1,120	1,251
Total	**1,542**	**2,468**	**2,633**

One person households are of special interest because they represent so large a proportion of the projected total net increase in households (Table 6) and make a major contribution to the downward revision of the projected increase in households compared with the 1992-based projections (Table 18). One person households are very heterogeneous. An analysis of the projected future increase and how it compares with past changes along with how the current projections differs from the previous projections has therefore to be considered in detail. As a starting point, Table 11 shows the projected and past number of one person households analysed by age according to whether they are nver married men and women or whether they are formerly married, that is divorced, legally married but separated or widowed.

The net increase in one person households that is projected between 1996 and 2021 is 2.70 million, slightly less that the estimated increase of 2.85 million between 1971 and 1996 (Table 6). Thus the projected increase is not out of line with past experience. However, Table 11 shows that the composition of the increase projected for 1996 - 2021 is very different from the composition of the increase between 1971 and 1996. The proportion of never married households is much higher between 1996 and 2021 and the proportion that is formerly married is correspondingly lower. The division of the increase in one person households between never married and formerly married that is projected for 1996 - 2021 is 74:26, compared with 41:59 in 1971 - 1996. Among the never married one person households there is a further difference between the two periods in the mix of ages.

Of the net increase between 1971 and 1996 in the number of never married women living as one person households, 70 per cent were under age 35; but this group represents only 17 per cent of the projected increase between 1996 and 2021. The reasons for this contrast in the increases in the numbers of never married and formerly married one person households, and in the ages of never married one person households, are complex. To provide some insights, more detailed analyses are made of never married and widowed one person households. Never married one person households predominate numerically in the projection period and among widowed one person households there is a very marked change of trend.

Table 12   Never Married Non-Cohabiting Men and Women in the Private Household Population (thousands)

	Age in years							
	20 - 29	30 - 34	35 - 44	45 - 54	55 - 64	65 - 74	75 & over	Total 20 & over
Men								
1971	1,447	172	266	227	180	104	33	2,428
1981	1,685	253	257	213	185	122	50	2,766
1991	2,248	378	378	210	178	127	63	3,581
1996	2,215	575	469	260	160	132	64	3,875
2001	2,091	648	685	279	155	108	70	4,036
2011	2,243	578	892	525	221	109	74	4,642
2021	2,171	648	891	762	482	187	91	5,232
Women								
1971	828	92	166	205	273	290	194	2,048
1981	1,055	125	132	139	185	230	213	2,079
1991	1,531	223	216	121	129	151	187	2,558
1996	1,554	341	285	148	109	131	160	2,726
2001	1,548	390	406	158	90	90	136	2,817
2011	1,719	404	564	308	124	70	97	3,286
2021	1,667	465	633	501	299	123	88	3,775

3d(i) Single (never married) one person households

The change in the number of never married one person households depends on the change in the number of non-cohabiting never married men and women in the private household population, their age distribution and the proportion of them in each age group that live as one person households (the one person representative rates). The estimated population in 1971, 1981, 1991 and 1996 and the projections for 2001, 2011 and 2021 are shown in Table 12. The figures in this table differ from Table D.8 because they are of the private household population in England, whereas Table D.8 shows projections of the total non-cohabiting never married population in England and Wales.

Up to 1996, the increase in the number of single non-cohabiting men and women was predominantly at ages under 35. But between 1996 and 2021, the majority of the projected increases are at ages 35 and over: 98 per cent for men, 77 per cent for women. The reasons for this increase are discussed in Annex D. First marriage rates have fallen slightly, with only a partial offset from more cohabitation. With the passage of time, these effects extend progressively to higher age groups.

The increases in the number of single non-cohabiting men and women interact with the rising proportions of them living alone. These proportions, past and projected are given in Table 13. They are not total household representative rates because they do not include lone parent households and "other multi-person" households.

Table 13	Proportions of Non-Cohabiting Never Married Men and Women Living as One Person Households (per cent)						
	Age in years						
	20 - 29	30 - 34	35 - 44	45 - 54	55 - 64	65 - 74	75 and over
Men							
1971	7	16	21	30	39	42	43
1981	10	27	31	39	50	55	55
1991	15	38	43	48	60	67	66
1996	18	43	49	52	63	71	70
2001	19	47	54	56	66	75	79
2011	21	53	63	63	72	81	81
2021	23	56	67	68	76	85	84
Women							
1971	6	17	22	32	47	52	53
1981	8	27	30	39	54	61	64
1991	12	31	38	46	60	69	72
1996	15	37	44	50	63	70	75
2001	15	38	46	54	65	73	78
2011	16	39	50	60	69	77	82
2021	17	38	51	64	72	79	83

In all age ranges distinguished in Table 13, the projected increase between 1996 and 2021 in the proportions of non-cohabiting never married men and women living alone as one person households is smaller (in percentage points) than the actual increase between 1971 and 1996. The very large projected increase between 1996 and 2021 in never married men living as one person households (Table 11) therefore comes primarily from the increase in the never married non-cohabiting population and not from an increased propensity to live alone. Of the projected increase between 1996 and 2021 of 1,347,000 never married men living as one person households, 1,120,000 are aged 35 and over. Of that increase, 380,000 (one third) is explained by projected increases between 1996 and 2021 in the proportion of non-cohabiting single men living as one person households and 740,000 (two thirds) by the increase in the number of non-cohabiting never married men. The projected increases in the proportions of never married men in their 20s living alone are small (5 percentage points) and in the under 35's as a whole. Young single men make only a small contribution to the projected increase in one person households.

The projected increases in the proportions of non-cohabiting never married women living as one person households are generally smaller than for men. The main reason for this in the younger age groups is that higher proportions of women than men are lone parents. Further up the age distribution, the increases in proportions of women living as one person households were smaller than for men and this difference has been projected into the future. The projected increase in the number of never married women living as one person households is nevertheless substantial, some 600,000 in the 35-74 age range. Some 120,000 is accounted for by increases in the proportions living as one person households, 480,000 (four-fifths of the total projected increase) by the growth between 1996 and 2021 in the number of never married non-cohabiting women.

3d(ii) Widows and widowers living alone as one person households

In the projection period there is a very marked change of trend in the number of widow one person households. Up until 1991 their number had risen rapidly since at least the early 1950's. There is then a small fall (estimated and projected) between 1991 and 2001 and then a steeper fall in the two following decades to 2021. The explanation for this trend lies wholly in the number of widows. As shown in Table 15, the proportion of widows living alone has risen strongly in the past and is projected to continue to do so, though at a slower rate. The fall in the number of widows after 1981 in place of the previous rise was demographic in origin. This was mainly as a result of falls in the numbers of births earlier in the century reducing the number of women reaching the ages where widowhood is common (in 1981 the 55-59 and higher age groups) . About 70 per cent of married men predecease their wives. Thus lower male mortality at higher ages results in women being widowed later. This is not fully offset by women living longer once widowed, as female longevity is not increasing at the same rate as male longevity (see Annex D). Widowers are fewer. Their number has levelled off but is not projected to fall, owing to the lower male mortality referred to above.

The past and projected numbers of widows and widowers analysed by age are shown in Table 14. Strictly speaking the numbers are of the non-cohabiting widows and widowers, but the numbers who cohabit are small. It is estimated that in 1996, 1.6 per cent of widows and 3.0 percent of widowers cohabited. More significant is that the table refers to the private household population and excludes residents of institutions such as residential care homes and nursing homes (see Annex E). A continued increase after 2001 in the proportion of widows that live in their own homes would raise the number of widows in the private household population and therefore the number of widow one person households.

The widowed population grew older between 1971 and 1996 and is projected to continue to do so between 1996 and 2021. Between 1971 and 1996 the number of widows in the private household population aged under 75 fell by 476,000 while the number aged 75 and over rose by 380,000. Between 1996 and 2021, the number of widows under 75 is projected to fall by a further 321,000 and the number aged 75 and over by 114,000. The number of widowers under 75 also fell between 1971 and 1996 and is projected to fall further between 1996 and 2021.

Table 14	Widows and Widowers Living in the Private Household Population (thousands)					
	Age in years					
	under 55	55 - 64	65 - 74	75 - 84	85 and over	Total
Men						
1971	60	117	205	175	50	608
1981	45	97	210	203	54	609
1991	38	84	201	227	67	617
1996	43	72	194	226	83	618
2001	44	71	166	232	94	608
2011	38	75	158	221	107	599
2021	29	68	170	233	118	618
Women						
1971	232	507	881	709	193	2,523
1981	182	429	896	851	243	2,602
1991	142	352	799	936	330	2,558
1996	121	285	738	897	385	2,425
2001	110	258	628	873	419	2,288
2011	86	245	542	754	426	2,053
2021	63	210	550	748	420	1,992

The proportion of widows and widowers in the private household population who were living alone rose quickly between 1971 and 1996. This continued a trend, which can be observed back to 1951 and may have begun earlier. This trend is to continue but at a slower rate as the percentage is now very high. The proportions are shown in Table 15 but are not overall household representative rates as they only refer to one person households.

Table 15	Proportion of Widows and Widowers Living as One Person Households by Age				Number of widowed one person household (thousands)
	Age in years				
	55 - 64	65 - 74	75 - 84	85 and over	
Men					
1971	52	58	54	40	305
1981	56	71	71	61	388
1991	62	75	80	75	447
1996	62	75	82	81	458
2001	63	77	85	87	468
2011	65	79	90	94	488
2021	66	81	92	97	524
Women					
1971	55	63	57	40	1,373
1981	57	73	73	56	1,700
1991	62	76	82	73	1,875
1996	62	78	84	78	1,842
2001	63	80	87	84	1,819
2011	67	83	92	92	1,730
2021	69	86	94	95	1,744

The rising proportions of widows and widowers living as one person households are partly the consequence of rising overall household representative rates at each age and partly more living alone and fewer as lone parents (mostly with only non-dependent children) and other kinds of "other multi-person households". Also very important has been the changing number of widows and widowers. Increasing male longevity is one of the reasons for the fall in the number of widows (Table D.4 of Annex D); but more important is the changing age structure of the population due to falling births year by year between 1910 and 1930. Increasing proportions of widows living alone only partly offset the effect of the diminishing size of the widowed population.

The projected rise in the proportion of widows living as one person households offsets much of the reduction in the total number of widows in the private household population. Between 1996 and 2021 the total number of widows is projected to fall by 433,000 but the number of widow one person households by only 98,000. How this fall compares with the 1992-based projections is discussed in a later section.

4. Sensitivity of the national household projections to changes in assumptions

The components from which the household projections are derived incorporate a large number of separate assumptions about demographic trends. The assumptions about the pace of these trends are considered to be the most appropriate for projection purposes, but there is inevitably a degree of uncertainty, which increases with distance in time. The Government accepted the recommendation of the House of Commons Select Committee on the Environment, Transport and the Regions that the 1996-based household projections should be accompanied by measures of their sensitivity to small changes in the assumptions. Measures of sensitivity are accordingly presented in this report.

Three groups of assumptions are distinguished:

(a) the assumptions for the official projections of the population, about future births, deaths and migration (Annex C).

(b) the assumptions embodied in the official projections of marital status and cohabitation (Annex D).

(c) the projected future changes in household representative rates that are applied to projections of the population analysed by sex, age, marital status and cohabitation.

Strictly speaking, there are assumptions also about the institutional population. No measure of sensitivity is shown for these assumptions, because their effect is so small in comparison with the other sets of assumptions.

Some indications are also given about the sensitivity of future increases in numbers of households to changes in economic conditions. These are not measures of sensitivity of the official household projections to, for example, the future rate of rise of real incomes, because no explicit assumptions about the economic future are required for the projection method. Nevertheless, the sensitivity to economic trends of the future increase in households is clearly important.

The official population projections include variant projections based on higher and lower assumptions for the principal projections about births, deaths and migration (*National population projections 1996-based* PP2 No 21 (1999), Chapter 4). Similarly, the official projections of marital status (Shaw (1999)) include variant projections with higher and lower assumptions about marriage and divorce rates and the projections of cohabitation (Shaw and Haskey (1999)) also include high and low variants. The assumptions for these higher and lower variants were chosen for the purposes of demographic analysis. They are used here because they have an official provenance. The high and low variants and how they differ are described in Annex G. The difference in the projected number of households in 2021 obtained by substituting a high or low variant for the principal projection is shown in Table G.7 of Annex G.

Sensitivities to assumptions about the number of households that will form from a projected private household population of a given size and composition (including marital status and proportions cohabiting) are different in concept from the demographic sensitivities. Household representative rates are specific for sex, age, marital status and cohabitation, so variant assumptions about representative rates must make sense within this detail. By definition, household representative rates cannot exceed 100 per cent, so for many categories of the private household population significantly higher variants are not possible. Lower variants are not subject to this logical constraint. But there is an important behavioural constraint in that representative rates for a specific group in a given year are related to the rates in previous years. The household representative rate for widows aged 80-84 in 2011, for example, must be compatible with the rate for those aged 75-79 in 2006. This is an aspect of the relationship of household representative rates to the life cycle, discussed in Annex B as an integral part of the projection. Lower variant assumptions that implied that people would be forced to give up living independently without assignable cause would not give a meaningful indication of the sensitivity of the household projections to the assumptions about the future course of household representative rates. Young and middle aged never married non-cohabiting men and women are the main group where there is room for higher and lower variant assumptions about household representative rates. The effect of a small change in household representative rates for this group is exemplified by an increase one half per cent faster or slower per five year period. That is, household representative rates $1\frac{1}{2}$ percentage points higher or lower than the main assumption by 2011 and $2\frac{1}{2}$ percentage points higher or lower by 2021.

Table 16	Sensitivities of the Official Household Projections to Small Changes in Demographic Assumptions (thousands)		
		2021	**Notes**
Fertility (plus or minus 0.2 children per woman in the long term)		+40/-60	(a)
Mortality (minus 1.0 years or plus years (approx.) on the increase between 1996 and 2021 in the expectation of life at birth for males(*))		-180/+160	(b)
Migration (plus or minus 40,000 a year)		+450/-410	(c)
Marriage (plus or minus 15% in first marriage rates, 10% in remarriage rates)		-100/+110	(d)
Divorce (plus or minus 10 per cent divorce rate in the long term)		+60/-60	(e)
Cohabitation (plus or minus 20 per cent (never married) or 10 per cent (formerly married) in the long term in proportions cohabiting)		-180/+180	(f)
Household representative rates of young and middle aged single men and women (plus or minus $1\frac{1}{2}$ per cent by 2011 and $2\frac{1}{2}$ per cent by 2021)		+201/-201	

Notes: (*) Figures for females are slightly different - see Annex G

(a) Higher fertility produces more projected households

(b) Higher mortality (lower life expectancy) produces fewer projected households

(c) Higher migration produces more projected households

(d) Higher marriage rates produce fewer projected households

(e) Higher divorce rates produce more projected households

(f) Higher proportions cohabiting produce fewer projected households

The sensitivities of the projected number of households in 2021 to changes in the demographic assumptions and in the projected rate of rise of household representative rates among young and middle aged non-cohabiting men and women are shown in Table 16.

The direction of the effect on the projected number of households from changes in the assumptions about births, deaths and migration is automatic. But the direction of the effects of changes in the assumptions about marriages, divorces and cohabitation depends on the household membership rates of single and divorced men and women. Sufficiently high proportions of unmarried non-cohabiting men and women live independently for more marriages to produce a net reduction in households and more divorces an increase. For the same reason, higher proportions cohabiting reduce the number of separate households, though the effect is much less than a net reduction of one household for each cohabiting couple. Table G.6 and G.7 in Annex G suggest that the net reduction in the number of households is about one third of the increase in the number of cohabiting couples (with no change assumed in the number of married couples).

The demographic variants and the household projection sensitivities derived from them are treated as substantially independent. Selecting the low variant assumption about migration, for example, would have no implications for whether the lower assumption about mortality was more likely than the central or higher assumption, or whether the lower assumption about marriage rates was therefore to be preferred. Sensitivities are presented in Table 16 for seven key assumptions. There are three values for each sensitivity - central, higher or lower; so the number of different combinations that are possible is 3 to the power of seven, i.e. 2,187. The sensitivities in Table 16 are not additive, since they interact. More migrants of marriageable age, for instance, increase the effect of differences in marriage rates. In addition they are not additive with the economic sensitivities given below in Table 17.

The status of alternative assumptions about future economic conditions is different. The projection process does not include explicit assumptions about the future course of real incomes, unemployment and house prices, so variant assumptions analogous to the assumptions about migration or marriage rates cannot be studied. Real incomes, real interest rates and unemployment could affect, for instance, the demand to live independently instead of remaining a member of someone else's household and the ability to afford to do so. But how the rate of increase in the number of separate households is affected by economic conditions in the medium to long term is a question that cannot be answered from within the present household projection system.

Some evidence can be provided by the household projection component of the economic model of demand and need for social housing prepared for DETR by the Department of Applied Economics at Cambridge University (DAE). The increase in household numbers for the private household population is modelled for three age groups, 15-29, 30-59 and 60 and over. The data used for this analysis was taken from the General Household Survey. The main advantage of using this data is that it includes significant variation in the main macro economic variables and allows a model of household formation to be estimated with the key macro determinants of household formation. The main disadvantages of using this data is that it will not allow for all of the demographic factors and a limited number of observations and the sample size precludes finer disaggregation by age or household type.

The official population projections provide the population subdivided by age group. The estimates of household formation in the DAE model are based on these population projections, but excluding the institutional population, which is calculated from rates, based on the 1991 Census of Population.

The growth rate in the total households for each of the three age bands are projected by means of equations in which the explanatory variables include a range of economic variables, notably real consumers' expenditure (as a proxy of real income), unemployment and real interest rates. The equations, along with other parts of the DAE model, were used to derive the sensitivity of household numbers to different assumptions about the annual increase in real consumers' expenditure, unemployment and real interest rates. The changes reflect how much household formation will change over 25 years from 1996 for a 1 per cent change throughout the period in unemployment or interest rates or 0.25 per cent for economic growth. Fuller details are given in Annex G. Sensitivities to differences in economic assumptions as calculated from the model are given in Table 17.

Table 17	Sensitivities of Future Numbers of Households in 2021 to Economic Assumptions (DAE Model) (thousands)		
		Higher	Lower
GDP : Growth of real income (plus or minus 0.25 per cent a year)		+190	-150
Level of unemployment (plus or minus 1 percentage point)		-20	+30
Real interest rates (plus or minus 1 percentage point)		-230	+260

There are some points to note about these estimates. First, the economic sensitivities are not additive because the economic variables are to some extent related and cannot be assumed to move independently. The economic factors may also be related to some of the demographic factors. Thus for these reasons it may be misleading to add any of the economic changes to the demographic changes. Second, the changes in Table 17 indicate that the scale of the sensitivities varies to some extent for increases and decreases in each of the economic factors. This variability reflects the asymmetric nature of the relationships in the DAE model. Finally, these sensitivities are likely to be less robust for larger changes in the variables. Simple extrapolation of the sensitivities in Table 17 for larger changes could produce misleading results. This is inherent in a model based on many estimated relationships where the degree of confidence about the estimates will depend on how far the economic assumptions are different from the historic past which is the basis for the estimated model. Moreover, unless the economic variables have an effect on marital status or cohabitation, their effect on the number of households must operate through household representative rates. There are some logical constraints on how these could vary in an upward direction. A similar constraint on downward movements arises from the large number of households less affected by unemployment or interest rates, for example economically inactive owner-occupiers who own outright. Extrapolating the sensitivities in Table 17 by assuming larger differences in economic growth and real interest rates could therefore produce unrealistic results.

5. Comparison between the 1996-based and the 1992 - based household projections

At national level, the comparison has two parts: a comparative table of the totals of households in 2016 analysed by type of household, with additional detail for selected household types, and an analysis of the difference by component causes. In the 1992-based projections, practically all of the change between 1991 and 2016 was projected change, apart from the population in 1992 and, in a very small way, the contribution of the 1992 Labour Force Survey (LFS) data to projecting household representative rates. In the 1996-based projection, the change between 1991 and 1996 is an estimated outturn and only the change between 1996 and 2016 is projection. Table 18 compares the projections by household type as in Table 1.

Table 18 Comparison of 1992-based and 1996-based Projections of Households in 2016 (thousands)			
	1992-based	**1996-based**	**Difference**
Married couple households	9,945	9,251	-694
Cohabiting couple households	1,579	2,660	+1,081
Lone parent households	1,257	1,296	+39
Other multi-person households	2,240	2,172	-68
One person households	8,577	7,934	-643
Total households	**23,598**	**23,313**	**-285**
Concealed couples	60	67	+7
Concealed lone parent families	83	89	+6

The reasons for the change in the projected number of married and cohabiting couple households lie primarily in the assumptions about marriage rates and in the proportions of never married men and women who cohabit. As noted in Annex D, the 1996-based projections are based on the assumption of a continuing increase in the proportion of never married men and women in each age group who cohabit. In the previous projections a constant proportion was assumed. The changes in the projected number of married couple households are more complex; at ages under 45 the 1996-based projected total is 587,000 lower and at ages 45-64 195,000 lower; but at ages 65 and over the 1996-based projection is 87,000 higher. Here the effect of assuming greater male longevity is observed (Annex C), which increases the number of married couples and holds down the increase in the number of widows and hence the number of widow one person households.

The difference in the projection of one person households warrants a more detailed analysis, not least because of the interest aroused by the large increase shown in the 1992-based household projections. Such an analysis, by sex and marital status, is shown in Table 19.

Table 19	Comparison of Projections of One Person Households in 2016 (thousands)					
	Male			**Female**		
	1992-based	**1996-based**	**Difference**	**1992-based**	**1996-based**	**Difference**
Never married						
Under 30	505	524	+19	226	316	+90
30 - 44	874	905	+31	355	468	+113
45 - 64	749	691	-58	454	398	-56
65 and over	228	188	-40	169	143	-26
Total	**2,355**	**2,307**	**-48**	**1,204**	**1,325**	**+121**
Formerly married						
Under 30	41	19	-22	24	12	-12
30 - 44	275	192	-83	113	95	-18
45 - 64	761	716	-45	669	602	-67
65 and over	839	771	-68	2,297	1,896	-401
Total	**1,916**	**1,697**	**-219**	**3,103**	**2,605**	**-498**

Because projected first marriage rates are lower in the 1996-based projections, the higher projection of cohabitation (Annex D) has not led to a downward revision in the projected number of younger never married one person households. The number of non-cohabiting never married men aged 20 - 29 and 30 - 44 in 2016 is projected to be slightly higher than in the 1992-based projections (by 86,000 and 57,000 respectively). In addition, the projected number of non-cohabiting single women is projected to be much higher (by 370,000 and 259,000 for the same age groups). Hence the larger difference for female than for male never married one person households shown in Table 19.

The projected reduction in one person households occurs primarily for older never married men and women and in particular for the formerly married. The difference between the 1996-based and 1992-based projections of formerly married men and women living as one person households can be divided into widowed and divorced and separated. This division is shown in Table 20.

Table 20	Analysis of Projected Number of Formerly married One Person Households in 2016 (thousands)		
	1992-based	**1996-based**	**Difference**
Widowed			
Male	540	524	-16
Female	2,174	1,744	-430
Divorced and Separated			
Male	1,376	1,173	-203
Female	928	861	-67

The downward revision to the projected number of widows in the population is the largest component of the overall reduction in the number of one person households.

The difference between the projections can be analysed into the effect of:

(i) different population projections;

(ii) different marital status projections;

(iii) different assumptions about the institutional population; and

(iv) different household representative rates.

Table 21 shows an analysis in these terms of the difference between the 1992-based and 1996-based projection for 2016. A similar analysis is made of the difference between the 1992-based projection for 1996 and the base estimate for that year for the 1996-based projections. As well as the mid-year population estimate for 1996 being higher than the 1992-based projection, there are differences in marital status (including cohabitation) and revisions to household representative rates, both owing to later information becoming available.

Table 21 Components of Difference Between the 1992-based and 1996-based Household Projections for 2016 (thousands)		
	1996	2016
Different population projections (Annex C)	+49	+159
Different projections of marital status and cohabitation (Annex D)	-34	-397
Different assumptions for projecting the institutional population (Annex E)	-2	+17
Different household representative rate projections	-4	-64
Total difference	**+9**	**-285**
A fuller analysis of these components of difference is in Annex F.		

The effect of the different projections of marital status (other than lower marriage rates and more cohabitation) is concentrated on one person households and is the main reason for the downward revision of over 600,000 in the projected number of one person households shown in Table 18. Some 400,000 of this are a downward revision of the number of widows (Table F.5). The reasons why the number of widows in the 1996-based projections of marital status is much lower than in the previous projection are discussed in Annex D.

As well as comparing the 1996-based projections of households with the immediately previous 1992-based projections, comparisons may be made with earlier projections, though not as far ahead. The first set of projections to reach to 2001 were the 1981-based projections, published in 1985 (see DoE (1985)). Subsequently there came the 1983-, 1985- and 1989-based projections published by DoE in 1986, 1988 and 1991 respectively. The projections from 1991 onwards are compared in Table 22.

Table 22 Official Household Projections for England: Comparison of Results (thousands)						
	1991	1996	2001	2006	2011	2016
1981-based	18,723	19,245	19,506	-	-	-
1983-based	18,661	19,205	19,481	-	-	-
1985-based	18,903	19,617	20,083	-	-	-
1989-based	19,036	19,910	20,603	21,217	21,983	-
1992-based	19,215 (a)	20,177 (a)	21,046	21,897	22,769	23,598
1996-based	19,213 (b)	20,186 (b)	20,992	21,733	22,519	23,313

Note: (a) Original outturn

(b) Revised outturn.

Source: DoE (1985), (1986), (1988), (1991) and (1995)

The population projections from which the household projections were derived were revised between each set of household projections, as were the marital status projections. Meriting comment is the way in which the projected slackening of the rate of increase in the number of households in the second half of the 1990s grew smaller and smaller. The slackening was expected as a result of the fall in births in the late 1960s and early 1970s as the "baby boom" came to an end. The projected increase between 1996 and 2001 was 50 per cent of the increase projected for 1991 - 96 in the 1981-based projections. It was 51 per cent in the 1983-based set, 65 per cent in the 1985-based projections, then 77 per cent, 90 per cent in the 1992-based projections and 83 per cent in the present 1996-based projections.

6. Regional household projections

The method for compiling the regional household projections is described in Annex B. The 1996-based regional projections are summarised for selected years in Table 23.

Table 23 1996-Based Projections of Households for Government Office Regions (thousands)						
	1971	1981	1991	1996	2011	2021
North East	910	978	1,048	1,080	1,135	1,167
North West (incl. Merseyside)	2,427	2,551	2,720	2,812	2,997	3,111
Yorkshire and the Humber	1,702	1,827	1,993	2,076	2,260	2,372
Sub total North	**5,040**	**5,356**	**5,761**	**5,968**	**6,392**	**6,650**
East Midlands	1,256	1,410	1,596	1,689	1,904	2,033
West Midlands	1,708	1,860	2,042	2,128	2,299	2,398
Sub total Midlands	**2,964**	**3,270**	**3,638**	**3,817**	**4,203**	**4,431**
East of England	1,502	1,764	2,035	2,166	2,494	2,701
London	2,705	2,635	2,841	3,002	3,377	3,645
South East	2,312	2,644	3,035	3,225	3,735	4,060
South West	1,427	1,638	1,903	2,010	2,017	2,515
Sub total South	**7,946**	**8,681**	**9,814**	**10,402**	**11,923**	**12,920**
England	**15,951**	**17,306**	**19,213**	**20,186**	**22,519**	**24,000**

To bring out more clearly some of the implications of the projections summarised in Table 23, a comparison is first made between the projected changes between 1996 and 2021 and the estimates of actual changes between 1971 and 1996, see Table 24. A comparison is then made between the 1992-based and 1996-based projections of the changes between 1991 and 2016, see Table 25.

Table 24 Projected Changes in Numbers of Households in 1996 - 2021 Compared With 1971 - 96 (thousands)			
	1971 - 1996	1996 - 2021	Difference
North East	+170	+87	-83
North West (including Merseyside)	+385	+299	-86
Yorkshire and the Humber	+374	+296	-78
Sub total North	**+928**	**+682**	**-246**
East Midlands	+433	+344	-92
West Midlands	+420	+270	-149
Sub total Midlands	**+853**	**+614**	**-239**
East of England	+664	+535	-129
London	+297	+643	+346
South East	+913	+835	-78
South West	+583	+505	-78
Sub total South	**+2,456**	**+2,518**	**+62**
England	**+4,235**	**+3,814**	**-421**

Table 25	1992-Based and 1996-Based Projections of Households and Adult Population 1991 - 2016 (thousands)					
	Households			Population (15 and over)		
	1992-based	1996-based	Difference	1992-based	1996-based	Difference
North East	+166	+106	-60	+66	+9	-57
N W (incl. Merseyside)	+483	+341	-142	+299	+126	-173
Yorkshire and the Humber	+387	+329	-58	+306	+270	-35
Sub total North	**+1,035**	**+776**	**-259**	**+669**	**+405**	**-264**
East Midlands	+418	+377	-41	+484	+456	-28
West Midlands	+367	+312	-55	+266	+231	-36
Sub total Midlands	**+785**	**+689**	**-96**	**+750**	**+657**	**-64**
East of England	+582	+567	-15	+647	+683	+36
London	+629	+680	+51	+413	+625	+212
South East	+807	+870	+63	+799	+1,027	+228
South West	+545	+513	-27	+625	+641	+16
Sub total South	**2,563**	**2,636**	**+73**	**2,485**	**2,977**	**+492**
England	**4,383**	**4,101**	**-282**	**+3,903**	**+4,062**	**+159**

Whereas in the quarter of a century from 1971 to 1996 some 42 per cent of the increase in the number of households was in the Midlands and North, only 34 per cent of the projected net increase between 1996 and 2021 is located there. The 8 percentage point difference is divided equally between the North and the Midlands. There is a most marked contrast between the estimated increase between 1971 and 1996 and the projected increase between 1996 and 2021 in London. London had 7 per cent of the net increase between 1971 and 1996 but has 17 per cent of the projected increase in the quarter of a century between 1996 and 2021. The share of the South outside London of the projected net increase in the number of households from 1996 to 2021 is 2 percentage points lower than its share of the actual increase in the previous quarter of a century. The distribution of the net increase is heavily dependent on migration, both within the United Kingdom and from overseas.

A comparison is made next between the 1996-based projections of household by region and the previous (1992-based) projections which they supersede. In many ways the projected increases in the number of households over time are of more interest than the levels, so the comparison is of the increases between 1991 and 2016, the end date for the 1992-based projections.

The 1996-based subnational population projections assume substantially more North to South migration than did the 1993-based projections that they superseded due to the analysis of more recent data. A high proportion of inward migration from overseas goes to London and the South East. Thus the larger volume of net inward migration assumed in the national population projection (Annex C) adds further to the projected population in the South East, especially London. As a consequence, the projected net increase in households in the North of England has been revised heavily downwards and raised in London and the South East. No actual fall in the number of households is projected in any of the regions.

Also meriting comment is what contribution the revised population projections made to the projected number of households at regional level. This is shown in Table 26, which divides the projected differences between the 1992-based and 1996-based household projections in the same way as in Table 21 for England as a whole.

Table 26 Projection of households in 2016: Components of Difference (thousands)					
	1992-based	Population projection	Marital status (a)	Institutional population	Household representative rates	1996-based
North East	1,213	-44	-12	+1	-4	1,154
Yorkshire and the Humber	2,380	-22	-37	+2	-1	2,322
North West (incl. Merseyside)	3,203	-67	-59	+3	-19	3,061
Sub total North	**6,796**	**-133**	**-108**	**+6**	**-24**	**6,537**
East Midlands	2,014	-2	-37	+2	-3	1,937
West Midlands	2,410	+8	-58	+2	-8	2,354
Sub total Midlands	**4,424**	**+6**	**-95**	**+3**	**-11**	**4,327**
East of England	2,617	+19	-32	+2	-3	2,602
London	3,471	+150	-87	+1	-14	3,505
South East	3,843	+107	-41	+3	-6	3,905
South West	2,448	+10	-34	+3	-6	3,520
Sub total South	**12,379**	**+286**	**-194**	**+8**	**-29**	**2,421**
England	**23,598**	**+159**	**-397**	**+17**	**-64**	**23,313**

Note (a)   Includes proportions cohabiting

Note: Figures do not always add to totals due to rounding

Growth in the number of households by household type
England: 1971-2021

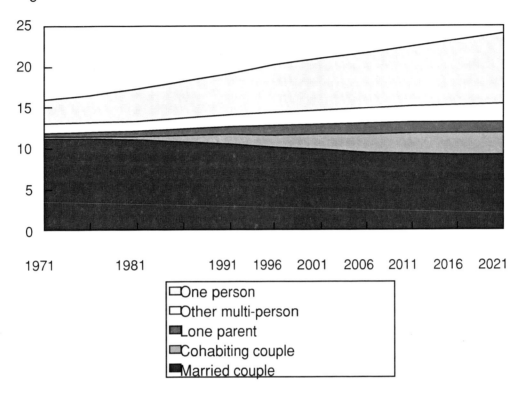

Number of households by household type
England: 1971, 1996 and 2021

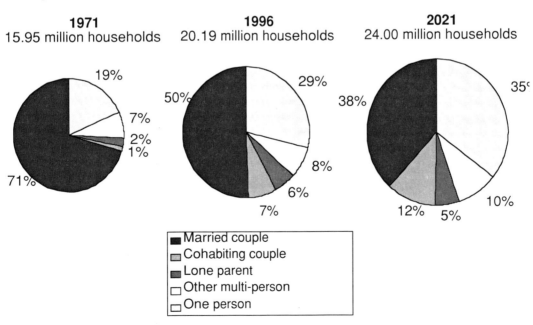

Married couple households by age of household representative
England: 1971, 1996 and 2021

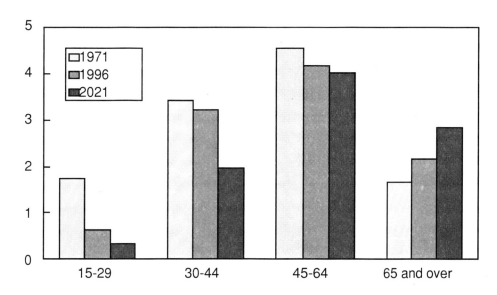

One person households by age of household representative
England: 1971, 1996 and 2021

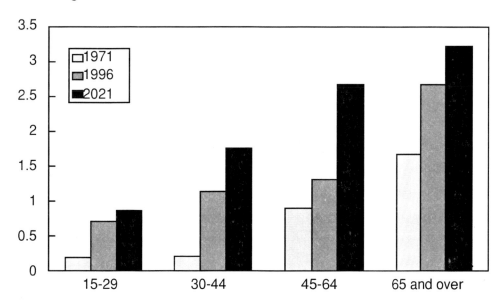

Table 1: Household projections: England (thousands)

	1981	1991	1996	2001	2006	2011	2016	2021
Household types:								
married couple	11,013	10,552	10,190	9,829	9,535	9,357	9,251	9,157
cohabiting couple	500	1,177	1,479	1,896	2,251	2,509	2,660	2,761
lone parent	625	975	1,168	1,258	1,293	1,299	1,296	1,288
other multi-person	1,234	1,367	1,543	1,676	1,836	2,012	2,172	2,286
one person	3,934	5,142	5,806	6,334	6,819	7,342	7,934	8,509
All households	**17,306**	**19,213**	**20,186**	**20,992**	**21,733**	**22,519**	**23,313**	**24,000**
Private household population	46,137	47,490	48,342	49,131	49,783	50,413	51,076	51,704
Average household size	2.67	2.47	2.40	2.34	2.29	2.24	2.19	2.15
Concealed couples	83	74	63	59	59	63	67	72
Concealed lone parents	82	91	89	87	89	90	89	88

Table 2: Household projections: Great Britain (thousands)

All households

	1981	1991	1996	2001	2006	2011	2016	2021
England	17,306	19,213	20,186	20,992	21,733	22,519	23,313	24,000
Wales	1,017	1,128	1,170	1,203	1,236	1,273	1,308	1,337
England and Wales	18,323	20,340	21,356	22,195	22,969	23,792	24,621	25,337
Scotland	1,854	2,052	2,136	2,215	2,287			
Great Britain	20,177	22,392	23,492	24,310	25,256			

Additional Source: National Assembly for Wales and Scottish Executive

Table 3: Household projections: Government Office Regions (thousands)

	1981	1991	1996	2001	2006	2011	2016	2021
England	**17,306**	**19,213**	**20,186**	**20,992**	**21,733**	**22,519**	**23,313**	**24,000**
North East	978	1,048	1,080	1,099	1,116	1,135	1,154	1,167
North West (including Merseyside)	2,551	2,720	2,812	2,875	2,932	2,997	3,061	3,110
Yorkshire and the Humber	1,827	1,993	2,076	2,136	2,195	2,260	2,322	2,372
East Midlands	1,410	1,596	1,688	1,764	1,833	1,904	1,973	2,033
West Midlands	1,860	2,042	2,128	2,189	2,243	2,299	2,354	2,398
East of England	1,764	2,035	2,166	2,284	2,388	2,494	2,602	2,701
London	2,635	2,841	3,002	3,128	3,245	3,377	3,520	3,645
South East	2,644	3,035	3,225	3,403	3,567	3,735	3,905	4,060
South West	1,638	1,903	2,010	2,115	2,214	2,317	2,421	2,515

Table 4: Household projections: by age gender and marital status of household representative (thousands)
England

	1981	1991	1996	2001	2006	2011	2016	2021
Male 15-29								
Married couple	1,312	970	627	376	313	328	345	336
Formerly married								
Cohabiting couple	34	51	36	20	15	16	17	17
Lone parent	6	6	5	3	2	2	2	2
Other-multi-person	10	14	10	6	5	6	6	6
One person	29	41	30	18	16	17	19	19
Never married								
Cohabiting couple	165	503	556	583	619	672	693	672
Lone parent	2	5	5	5	6	6	7	7
Other-multi-person	76	164	184	191	207	229	242	240
One person	172	344	407	417	446	491	524	519
All households	**1,806**	**2,098**	**1,860**	**1,618**	**1,628**	**1,767**	**1,854**	**1,818**
Male 30-44								
Married couple	3,573	3,454	3,221	3,039	2,650	2,209	1,955	1,961
Formerly married								
Cohabiting couple	126	243	260	270	241	193	163	162
Lone parent	51	55	66	70	63	50	42	42
Other-multi-person	40	75	93	101	93	75	62	61
One person	104	217	270	299	280	228	192	191
Never married								
Cohabiting couple	63	184	372	630	820	887	902	942
Lone parent	2	4	4	6	6	6	7	7
Other-multi-person	41	79	120	161	178	181	187	198
One person	149	309	480	680	812	865	905	965
All households	**4,149**	**4,620**	**4,887**	**5,254**	**5,143**	**4,694**	**4,415**	**4,530**
Male 45-64								
Married couple	4,150	4,003	4,170	4,191	4,276	4,363	4,218	4,020
Formerly married								
Cohabiting couple	72	140	185	232	286	325	327	302
Lone parent	41	31	45	51	57	62	59	51
Other-multi-person	107	130	172	216	261	298	307	303
One person	187	312	412	518	625	706	716	690
Never married								
Cohabiting couple	20	18	40	114	208	337	454	543
Lone parent	1	1	1	1	2	3	4	5
Other-multi-person	66	51	49	44	48	61	76	87
One person	175	208	236	260	334	490	691	887
All households	**4,817**	**4,895**	**5,312**	**5,628**	**6,098**	**6,644**	**6,851**	**6,890**

Table 4: Household projections: by age gender and marital status of household representatative (thousands) (continued) England								
	1981	1991	1996	2001	2006	2011	2016	2021
Male 65 and over								
Married couple	1,978	2,124	2,171	2,224	2,295	2,456	2,733	2,839
Formerly married								
Cohabiting couple	17	37	26	30	37	48	63	72
Lone parent	1	1	2	2	2	2	2	2
Other-multi-person	115	97	108	109	117	140	179	211
One person	376	469	515	555	600	670	771	855
Never married								
Cohabiting couple	3	0	3	17	25	32	41	50
Lone parent								
Other-multi-person	49	42	38	30	25	24	26	28
One person	95	127	138	134	133	148	188	236
All households	**2,634**	**2,898**	**3,001**	**3,100**	**3,234**	**3,519**	**4,002**	**4,294**

Table 4: Household projections: by age gender and marital status of household representatative (thousands) England								
	1981	**1991**	**1996**	**2001**	**2006**	**2011**	**2016**	**2021**
Female 15-29								
Formerly married								
Lone parent	63	110	83	53	44	48	52	52
Other-multi-person	2	3	2	1	1	1	1	1
One person	23	24	21	13	11	11	11	11
Never married								
Lone parent	59	203	250	279	311	345	365	360
Other-multi-person	29	41	49	51	54	59	62	61
One person	109	194	245	259	278	302	316	310
All households	**285**	**575**	**651**	**655**	**699**	**766**	**807**	**794**
Female 30-44								
Formerly married								
Lone parent	256	367	423	441	398	328	286	288
Other-multi-person	35	60	72	84	90	79	62	58
One person	47	111	130	142	135	113	95	93
Never married								
Lone parent	29	82	140	193	229	253	279	304
Other-multi-person	15	30	43	57	66	73	79	86
One person	73	151	251	336	399	436	468	498
All households	**454**	**802**	**1,059**	**1,253**	**1,318**	**1,282**	**1,270**	**1,328**
Female 45-64								
Formerly married								
Lone parent	107	99	131	142	156	170	161	133
Other-multi-person	234	267	317	375	447	516	551	559
One person	439	492	512	563	617	642	602	565
Never married								
Lone parent	6	6	9	10	13	20	26	30
Other-multi-person	24	19	22	21	26	37	53	68
One person	154	134	143	144	180	271	398	535
All households	**965**	**1,018**	**1,134**	**1,256**	**1,439**	**1,656**	**1,792**	**1,890**
Female 65 and over								
Formerly married								
Lone parent	2	2	3	3	3	4	4	5
Other-multi-person	331	262	237	213	206	225	270	310
One person	1,526	1,768	1,805	1,823	1,810	1,820	1,896	1,964
Never married								
Lone parent	0	0	0	0	0	0	0	0
Other-multi-person	61	34	25	17	12	9	8	9
One person	277	240	211	172	144	133	143	170
All households	**2,196**	**2,307**	**2,282**	**2,227**	**2,174**	**2,190**	**2,323**	**2,458**

Table 5: Household projections: Government Office Regions (thousands)							
	1981	**1991**	**1996**	**2001**	**2006**	**2011**	**2016**	**2021**

North East
Household types:

	1981	1991	1996	2001	2006	2011	2016	2021
married couple	622	577	549	522	499	482	469	455
cohabiting couple	22	51	62	76	88	96	99	101
lone parent	38	62	73	77	77	77	75	73
other multi-person	71	71	75	78	82	87	92	94
one person	224	287	320	346	369	393	419	443
All households	**978**	**1,048**	**1,080**	**1,099**	**1,116**	**1,135**	**1,154**	**1,167**
Private household population	2,611	2,571	2,568	2,547	2,522	2,502	2,487	2,474
Average household size	2.67	2.45	2.38	2.32	2.26	2.20	2.16	2.12
Concealed couples	3	2	2	2	2	2	2	2
Concealed lone parents	5	7	7	7	8	8	8	8

North West (including Merseyside)
Household types:

	1981	1991	1996	2001	2006	2011	2016	2021
married couple	1,600	1,478	1,409	1,341	1,285	1,246	1,217	1,191
cohabiting couple	58	145	179	224	261	286	299	306
lone parent	106	165	195	208	211	210	208	204
other multi-person	188	191	209	221	239	260	278	290
one person	598	742	821	881	936	994	1,058	1,119
All households	**2,551**	**2,720**	**2,812**	**2,875**	**2,932**	**2,997**	**3,061**	**3,110**
Private household population	6,855	6,788	6,790	6,772	6,744	6,722	6,713	6,705
Average household size	2.69	2.50	2.41	2.36	2.30	2.24	2.19	2.16
Concealed couples	10	8	6	6	5	5	5	5
Concealed lone parents	17	20	20	20	21	22	22	22

Yorkshire and the Humber
Household types:

	1981	1991	1996	2001	2006	2011	2016	2021
married couple	1,172	1,109	1,068	1,024	990	969	956	945
cohabiting couple	50	121	149	187	220	243	255	262
lone parent	67	102	120	127	129	129	127	125
other multi-person	114	124	140	153	168	182	194	201
one person	423	537	598	644	688	736	789	840
All households	**1,827**	**1,993**	**2,076**	**2,136**	**2,195**	**2,260**	**2,322**	**2,372**
Private household population	4,862	4,917	4,967	5,003	5,030	5,061	5,096	5,129
Average household size	2.66	2.47	2.39	2.34	2.29	2.24	2.19	2.16
Concealed couples	7	6	5	5	5	6	6	7
Concealed lone parents	10	11	10	10	10	10	10	10

Table 5: Household projections: Government Office Regions (thousands) (continued)							
	1981	1991	1996	2001	2006	2011	2016	2021

East Midlands
Household types:

	1981	1991	1996	2001	2006	2011	2016	2021
married couple	946	928	910	888	871	865	863	861
cohabiting couple	39	103	129	163	192	214	225	232
lone parent	45	72	87	93	95	95	94	93
other multi-person	85	97	112	125	140	155	167	175
one person	294	396	451	495	535	576	624	672
All households	**1,410**	**1,596**	**1,688**	**1,764**	**1,833**	**1,904**	**1,973**	**2,033**
Private household population	3,809	3,985	4,088	4,181	4,257	4,328	4,399	4,464
Average household size	2.70	2.50	2.42	2.37	2.32	2.27	2.23	2.20
Concealed couples	6	6	5	5	5	6	6	7
Concealed lone parents	6	7	7	7	7	7	7	7

West Midlands
Household types:

	1981	1991	1996	2001	2006	2011	2016	2021
married couple	1,234	1,172	1,128	1,082	1,042	1,015	995	976
cohabiting couple	48	119	148	187	219	241	254	262
lone parent	67	102	123	132	136	137	137	135
other multi-person	126	135	150	160	173	187	198	204
one person	385	514	580	629	672	719	771	821
All households	**1,860**	**2,042**	**2,128**	**2,189**	**2,243**	**2,299**	**2,354**	**2,398**
Private household population	5,132	5,206	5,254	5,280	5,294	5,307	5,325	5,342
Average household size	2.76	2.55	2.47	2.41	2.36	2.31	2.26	2.23
Concealed couples	12	11	9	9	9	10	11	12
Concealed lone parents	11	11	11	10	11	11	11	10

East of England
Household types:

	1981	1991	1996	2001	2006	2011	2016	2021
married couple	1,202	1,198	1,174	1,154	1,137	1,132	1,133	1,134
cohabiting couple	48	131	166	211	250	278	295	306
lone parent	54	82	100	109	114	115	115	115
other multi-person	104	122	142	158	176	196	216	232
one person	356	502	583	652	712	774	844	914
All households	**1,764**	**2,035**	**2,166**	**2,284**	**2,388**	**2,494**	**2,602**	**2,701**
Private household population	4,788	5,079	5,218	5,373	5,506	5,625	5,744	5,859
Average household size	2.71	2.50	2.41	2.35	2.31	2.26	2.21	2.17
Concealed couples	6	6	6	6	6	7	7	8
Concealed lone parents	6	7	7	7	6	6	6	6

Table 5: Household projections: Government Office Regions (thousands) (continued)								

	1981	1991	1996	2001	2006	2011	2016	2021
London								
Household types:								
married couple	1,439	1,260	1,185	1,105	1,037	989	956	932
cohabiting couple	112	191	244	332	408	464	500	528
lone parent	113	191	231	252	264	270	276	280
other multi-person	260	304	342	368	396	428	457	476
one person	711	895	1,000	1,070	1,141	1,227	1,331	1,429
All households	**2,635**	**2,841**	**3,002**	**3,128**	**3,245**	**3,377**	**3,520**	**3,645**
Private household population	6,689	6,790	6,973	7,117	7,241	7,375	7,514	7,641
Average household size	2.54	2.39	2.32	2.28	2.23	2.18	2.14	2.10
Concealed couples	20	18	15	12	11	11	12	13
Concealed lone parents	11	11	10	9	9	8	8	8
South East								
Household types:								
married couple	1,735	1,741	1,703	1,667	1,638	1,624	1,620	1,616
cohabiting couple	80	202	257	330	394	441	472	494
lone parent	83	120	146	158	163	163	162	160
other multi-person	175	200	232	258	288	323	358	387
one person	572	771	887	990	1,084	1,183	1,294	1,402
All households	**2,644**	**3,035**	**3,225**	**3,403**	**3,567**	**3,735**	**3,905**	**4,060**
Private household population	7,098	7,534	7,745	7,985	8,195	8,384	8,570	8,749
Average household size	2.69	2.48	2.40	2.35	2.30	2.25	2.20	2.16
Concealed couples	11	11	9	9	9	9	10	10
Concealed lone parents	10	10	10	10	10	9	9	9
South West								
Household types:								
married couple	1,062	1,089	1,065	1,047	1,036	1,036	1,042	1,047
cohabiting couple	44	115	145	185	220	246	261	270
lone parent	52	78	93	100	103	103	103	102
other multi-person	110	123	141	156	174	194	212	228
one person	371	498	566	627	681	738	803	869
All households	**1,638**	**1,903**	**2,010**	**2,115**	**2,214**	**2,317**	**2,421**	**2,515**
Private household population	4,292	4,620	4,739	4,874	4,993	5,107	5,226	5,340
Average household size	2.62	2.43	2.36	2.30	2.26	2.20	2.16	2.12
Concealed couples	7	6	6	6	6	6	7	7
Concealed lone parents	7	7	7	7	7	7	7	7

Table 6: Household projections: Standard Statistical Regions (thousands)

All households

	1981	1991	1996	2001	2006	2011	2016	2021
England	17,306	19,213	20,186	20,992	21,733	22,519	23,313	24,000
Northern Region	1,155	1,245	1,285	1,311	1,335	1,362	1,387	1,407
Yorks and Humberside Region	1,827	1,993	2,076	2,136	2,195	2,260	2,322	2,372
East Midlands Region	1,410	1,596	1,688	1,764	1,833	1,904	1,973	2,033
East Anglia Region	701	832	885	938	986	1,036	1,086	1,132
South East Region	6,342	7,078	7,507	7,877	8,214	8,571	8,942	9,273
Greater London	2,635	2,841	3,002	3,128	3,245	3,377	3,520	3,645
Rest of South East	3,707	4,238	4,505	4,749	4,969	5,193	5,421	5,629
South West Region	1,638	1,903	2,010	2,115	2,214	2,317	2,421	2,515
West Midlands Region	1,860	2,042	2,128	2,189	2,243	2,299	2,354	2,398
North West Region	2,373	2,523	2,607	2,662	2,713	2,771	2,828	2,870

ANNEX A
Definitions and concepts

A **household** is defined as in the 1981 and 1991 Census as:

- One person living alone, or
- A group of people who share common housekeeping or a living room.

This differs from the definition used in the 1971 and earlier censuses. Previously, people who catered separately were to be counted as separate households even if they shared a living room. For example, three people each with a room of their own and catering separately, but sharing a sitting room or living room would, under the 1971 census definition, have been counted as three "one person households", but would in 1981 and 1991 be counted as one "other multi person household".

A **family** is defined as in the 1991 Census as:

a.   a married couple with or without their never married child(ren) including childless married couples (**married couple families**);

b.   a cohabiting couple with or without their never married child(ren) including childless cohabiting couples (**cohabiting couple families**);

c.   a father or mother together with his or her never married child(ren) (**lone parent families**); or

d.   grandparent(s) with grandchild(ren) if there are no apparent parents of the grandchild(ren) usually resident in the household.

Families of type (d) are classified as a married couple family, cohabiting couple family or lone parent family as appropriate. This definition differs from that used in the 1981 and earlier censuses in its inclusion of cohabiting couple families. In the context of the household projections, the term "child" is taken to refer only to a dependent child, that is one aged 0-15; or aged 16-18, never married and in full time education. A lone parent living with his/her non-dependent children (only) would not therefore constitute a lone parent family. This contrasts with the 1989-based and earlier projections where the "children" could be of any age. It should be noted that the terms "household" and "family" are not synonymous. A household may contain no families (for example one person living alone, or a household of unrelated, non cohabiting adults), or it may consist of one or more families with or without additional non family members.

Households are sub divided into five **household types**:

a.   **Married couple household**: a household which contains one or more married couple families;

b.   **Cohabiting couple household**: a household which contains one or more cohabiting couple families, but no married couple families;

c.   **Lone parent household**: a household which contains one or more lone parent families, but no married couple or cohabiting couple families;

d.   **Other multi person household**: a multi person household that is neither a married couple household nor a cohabiting couple household nor a lone parent household.

Examples include, lone parents with only non dependent children, brothers and sisters and unrelated (and non-cohabiting) adults sharing a house or flat;

e.   **One person household**: a person living alone who shares neither housekeeping nor a living room with anyone else.

The definitions (a), (b), (c) and (d) are as in the 1992-based projections, but differ from earlier projections. The category of "married couple household" includes households which contain a married couple but in which an individual other than the husband and wife was recorded as the head of household by the census. An example would be a married couple living with an elderly relative, where the relative was entered first on the census form, for instance because he or she owned the house. The definition of "lone parent household" is restricted to exclude lone parents with only non-dependent children: in most contexts, the interest in lone parents is in lone parents with dependent children. Lone parents with only non-dependent children belong to the "other multi- person household" category. Cohabiting couples are distinguished as a separate household type. Before the 1992-based projections, cohabiting couples were included among lone parent households and "other households" (now called "other multi-person households") according to whether the household included children and whose children they were. The definition of "one person households" is the same as in all previous projections.

The **household membership** variable has eleven categories. All household members are classified to one (and only one) of these categories:

a.   **Married couple household representative**: the eldest married couple husband in the household;

b.   **Cohabiting couple household representative**: the eldest male cohabiter in a cohabiting couple household;

c.   **Lone parent household representative**: the eldest male lone parent in a lone parent household, if any; the eldest female lone parent if not.

d.   **Other multi-person household representative**:

  (i) in an other multi person household containing a lone parent (of non-dependent children only), the eldest lone parent if any; the eldest female lone parent if not; or

  (ii) in an other multi-person household containing no lone parents, the eldest male, if any; the eldest female if not.

e.   **One person household representative**;

f.   **Husband in a concealed married couple family**: any husband in a married couple family who is not included in (a);

g.   **Male cohabiter in a concealed cohabiting family**: any cohabiting male who is not included in (b);

h.   **Parent in a concealed lone parent family**: any lone parent who is not included in (c);

i.   **Wife in married couple family**;

j.   **Female cohabiter**;

k.   **Other individual.**

Individuals in categories (a) to (e) are household representatives, in the sense that each household contains one person (and only one) in one of these groups and the total number of households is equal, by definition, to the number of individuals in these groups. The categories to which a household's representative belongs defines the type of household.

For which types of household a man or woman can be household representative depends on legal marital status and whether he or she is cohabiting unmarried.

	Male				Female		
Married	**Widowed**	**Divorced**	**Single**	**Married**	**Widowed**	**Divorced**	**Single**
Not cohabiting							
MCH	LPH	LPH	LPH	LPH	LPH	LPH	LPH
LPH	OMPH	OMPH	OMPH	OMPH	OMPH	OMPH	OMPH
OMPH	OPH	OPH	OPH	OPH	OPH	OPH	OPH
OPH							
Cohabiting							
CCH	CCH	CCH	CCH	none	none	none	none

MCH   =   Married couple household
CCH   =   Cohabiting couple household
LPH   =   Lone parent household
OMPH =   Other multi-person household
OPH   =   One person household

Only a legally married man can be the household representative for a married couple household. A cohabiting man, whatever his marital status, can be household representative only for a cohabiting couple household. A cohabiting woman cannot be a household representative. A legally married woman can be a household representative only if not usually resident in the same household as her husband. This does not necessarily imply that she is separated, in the sense that her marriage has broken down. The same applies when a legally married man is household representative for a household which is not a married couple household.

The rationale for the concept of the household representative was explained in *Projections of Households in England to 2016* (page 61). In brief, the main reason was to avoid the distortions that could arise from inconsistencies among census form fillers about who was entered as "first person". In household interview surveys, the interviewer follows specified rules about which member of a household is designated head of the household (HoH). The rules for selecting the household representative select, in a high proportion of instances, the same person who would be selected as HoH according to interview survey rules, but not in all instances. In interview surveys, the HoH is the person whose name the accommodation is owned or rented, with rules of precedence if it is owned or rented in the names of two persons or more. However, who is household representative is not affected by who owns or rents the accommodation. Thus the husband in an elderly couple who live with their son and daughter-in-law (for example) is the household representative; but the son is HoH if he and his wife own the house. Differences between the household head and the household representative do not affect the number of households in the population. They affect the way households in the census population are classified, not their number. They may, however, affect the projection, because the rates of change of the population in different age/sex/marital status categories are not the same. Selecting as household representative a member of a quickly growing population category instead of a member of a group that is increasing more slowly will raise the projected increase in the number of households, other things being equal.

Any family other than that of the household representative is referred to as a **concealed family**. These are categorised as:

a.   **Concealed married couple family:** a married couple family living within a household where another person is household representative;

b.   **Concealed cohabiting couple family**: a cohabiting couple family living within a household where another person is household representative;

c.   **Concealed lone parent family**: a lone parent with dependent child(ren) living within a household where another person is household representative.

The number of individuals in categories (f), (g) and (h) on page 50 determines the number of concealed families of each type. This publication presents combined totals for concealed married couple families and concealed cohabiting couple families, the combined group being referred to as "concealed couple families".

Household representative rate: the proportion of a population group which are household representatives (sometimes expressed as a percentage). The population groups are defined for the 1996-based national projections and sub national projections according to sex, age (15 bands from 15-19 to 85 and over), legal marital status (married widowed, divorced, single) and cohabitational status: hence there are 240 population groups and 240 representative rates in total.

Household membership rate: the proportion of a population group who are of a particular household membership type. Eleven household membership types are defined, but some of these categories are necessarily empty for some population groups (for example, the category of "married couple wives" must be empty for all male groups). Taking into account these structural zeros, there are 825 defined household membership rates for each area.

Marital status factors: the proportions of a population who are (separately) married, widowed, divorced and single, cross analysed by whether cohabiting or not. There are eight marital status categories.

Resident population: all persons who usually live in the area, whatever their nationality. Members of HM and non-UK Armed forces in England are included on a residential basis. HM forces stationed outside England are not included. Students are taken to be resident at their term time address.

Institutional population: the population wholly resident in communal establishments, such as residential care homes, nursing homes and long stay hospitals. Resident staff as well as other residents are included.

Private household population: the resident population minus the institutional population.

ANNEX B
Methodology and sources of data

The method

The household projections are compiled by applying projected household membership rates to a projection of the private household population disaggregated by age, sex and marital/cohabitational status and summing the resulting projections of household representatives. This technique is substantially the same as the headship rate method which was first applied in this country by the Registrar General in the Housing Report of the 1931 census and subsequently developed in the Housing Report of the 1951 census and in Walkden (1961). Projection into the future of past rates of change of headship rates was first employed in the household projections produced by the Ministry of Housing and Local Government in 1968 and described fully in Allnutt, Cox and Mullock (1970). Those projections and all subsequent household projections published by the Department of the Environment up to and including the 1989-based projections published in 1991 (DoE, 1991), were in terms of legal marital status and took no explicit account of unmarried cohabitation. The 1992-based projections took explicit account of cohabitation and the present 1996-based projection do so in the same way.

The household projections are compiled through a six stage process:

(a)   the resident population is projected by the Government Actuary's Department (GAD) at national level and by the Office for National Statistics (ONS) for sub national areas of England. The latest household projections utilise the 1996-based national population projections which are summarised in Annex C. The subnational population projections are also 1996-based.

(b)   the marital status of the population is projected by GAD. This projection is made for England and Wales combined. It projects the population by legal (de jure) marital status (within sex and age) cross analysed by whether or not cohabiting. The proportions cohabiting in 1996 were estimated by ONS and projected for future years by GAD. This cross analysis is described in Annex D. The marital status projection is at national level only. Estimates of marital status in future years at subnational level are made by applying national/local differentials in marital status from the 1991 census to projected marital status factors.

(c)   the institutional population is projected by DETR from the 1991 census and information from the Department of Health about residents in residential care homes from 1991 to 1996. At ages under 75, the number of residents in institutions is kept constant at 1991 levels in each sex/age/marital status category. The marital status classification groups individuals into de jure categories only, as members of the institutional population do not cohabit by definition (resident staff with self contained accommodation are not part of the institutional population). In the 75-79, 80-84 and 85 and over age bands, the proportion of the population in each category resident in communal establishments is assumed to fall slowly from 1996 to 2001 and after that remain constant. Details of the 1996-based projection of the institutional population are in Annex E.

(d)   the institutional population is subtracted from the total resident population projection to leave the private household projection, analysed by sex, age and marital status (cross classified by cohabitation status) in the years required for household projections.

(e)   within each age/sex/marital cum cohabitational status category, household membership rates are projected from historical data derived from censuses and (at national level) Labour Force Survey (LFS) data. The projected household membership rates are then multiplied by the appropriate private household population projection.

(f)   projections for sub national areas are initially made independently of the national projections, but are subsequently adjusted for consistency with the national projection. Similarly, projections for sub regional areas are adjusted for consistency with the regional projections. These adjustment processes are termed "regional controlling".

Data sources

The data sources used for projecting household membership rates are a special analysis of a 10 per cent sample of the 1991 Census; the ONS Longitudinal Study samples from the 1971 and 1981 Censuses and the Labour Force Survey (LFS) from 1992 to 1997. The Labour Force Survey is considered the best available source of data about household membership rates after the 1991 Census. The way in which the 1971 and 1981 ONS Longitudinal Study samples and the 1991 Census sample were used to estimate comparably defined household membership rates for 1971, 1981 and 1991 was described fully in Annex B of *Projections of Households in England to 2016*. These household membership rates were used without change in the 1996-based household projections, so the description of them is not repeated here.

The Labour Force Survey has been used to extend the time series of household representative rates beyond the most recent available Census year. Compared with the Census 10 per cent sample, the Labour Force Survey samples are small, less than 1 per cent of the population. To minimise the effect of any systematic bias, the LFS data for 1992 - 97 have been adjusted to reflect the discrepancies between Census and LFS data in 1991. Because of the smaller sample used in the LFS, LFS household representative rates are calculated only by age and sex. Fully disaggregated household membership rates for 1992 to 1997 are produced by projecting Census data and then controlling the results to be consistent with the LFS based age/sex membership rates. These household membership rates are then used in conjunction with the Census data for national projections of household representative rates.

Projection method for household representative rates

Household representative rates in future years are projected from time trends estimated from the census based values for 1971, 1981 and 1991 and then the values from the Labour Force Survey. The "life cycle" method (Corner 1992) is used. This method makes used of the fact that the household membership rates in a particular cohort (defined by age) will vary smoothly with time. Furthermore, the changes in a particular rate in a given cohort will be the result of effects such as leaving the parental home, marriage and mortality, which are strongly dependent on the stage of the cohort's life cycle. It follows that, for each household membership status and marital status, plots of the cohort's membership rates against its age will have shapes which are recognisably similar for all cohorts. The projection method models this characteristic development of membership rates within cohorts as life cycle curves, which are assumed to undergo only trend changes in shape from cohort to cohort.

In practice, the household membership rates are modelled in terms of cohort birth date and cohort age by a two dimensional curve fitting method which makes a maximum likelihood fit to the available membership rate data. This method automatically weights data points according to sample size so that, for example, rates calculated for a small population group or from the LFS based data sets (which have comparatively small sampling fractions) are not given undue weight in determining the membership rate projections. In addition, explicit weights are applied for other purposes. An exponential weighting system is used to give greater weight to more recent data and further variations in the weights are incorporated to allow for uncertainties arising from definitional modifications and the errors introduced by estimation procedures such as those used in forming LFS based data sets.

Projection by time trend is appropriate where the observed changes are the result of numerous influences whose effects cannot be estimated separately. With only three census data points, the possible effects of economic variables such as real income, unemployment rates and mortgage rates cannot be distinguished one from another by statistical means, or together be distinguished from the effects of social changes. Upward trends in household membership rates and headship rates have been very long established. Rising trends are evident for the 1960s and 1950, as well as the 1980s and 1970s. Nothing is in view that could reasonably be expected to cause changes of trend in this respect, though of course the projected rising trends in individual household membership rates slow down as the maximum limit of 100 per cent is approached.

Medium term and longer term trends are the basis of the projections of households and of the underlying projections of population and marital status (Annexes C and D). In the shorter term there can be fluctuations around these trends. Such fluctuations are outside the scope of the projections, which can depict only medium term trends.

Regional controlling

Separate household projections are made independently for each projection area. This gives rise to inconsistencies, in the sense that the projected number of households in a given area is not normally equal to the sum of the household projections for its constituent sub areas. This problem stems from the non linearity of the household membership rate model and from the use of LFS-based data for England and Wales. A similar situation arises regarding private household population projections, originating in the division of the age/sex groups by marital status. In addition, the non-linearity of the projection method is such that unadjusted the projections will not normally have equal numbers of male and female cohabiters, or of husbands and wives in married couples.

The purpose of the regional controlling procedure is to adjust the household projections so that all of these consistency conditions are achieved. At the same time, it must maintain the age/sex resident population projections made by GAD and ONS. To accomplish this task, a "top down" procedure is used. The separate projections for England and for Wales are first modified to agree with those for the combined area of England and Wales. At the next stage, the projections for the English Regions are calibrated to the controlled projections for England. This procedure is continued down the "tree", the controlled projections for each area being used to calibrate the projections of its sub areas. Given the interdependence of the various constraints which apply, it is not possible to achieve consistency with a simple scaling technique. A mathematical optimisation method was used in the 1989-based and earlier projections to accomplish the controlling, but this approach was replaced in the 1992-based projections by a technique which is a generalisation of the scaling approach, which is retained in the present 1996-based projection.

ANNEX C
National population projections

This annex summarises the main features of the 1996-based projections of the population of England, from which projections of households are derived. Table 4 of the main report shows that three quarters of the projected net increase in households between 1996 and 2021 is arithmetically the consequence of the increase in the size of the population and changes in its age structure. The 1996-based population projections are therefore discussed in some detail, including the differences from the 1992-based projections. As noted in the Introduction, many of the features of household projections that have tended to attract most comment are in reality directly referrable to the population projections.

The 1996-based national population projections, like their predecessors, were produced by the Government Actuary's Department (GAD) from the 1996-based population as estimated by the Office for National Statistics (ONS) and assumptions about future births, deaths and migration decided by an inter-departmental committee of representatives of interested Government Departments. The projections appeared in summary form in a ONS First Release in November 1997 and in more detail in C Shaw "1996 based National Population Projections", *Population Trends* No 91, March 1998. Full details were published by the Office for National Statistics in *National population projections 1996-based*, Series PP2 No 21 in 1999. This annex deals with the population projections for England, as these are the projections on which the English household projections depend. The international migration assumption, however, relates to the United Kingdom in the first instance and so is described in UK terms.

The population projection for England summarised

The 1996-based population is summarised in Table C.1, divided by age into under 15, 15-44, 45-59, 60-74 and 75 and over.

Table C.1 Summary of Projection of Population for England (thousands)						
Age	1996 (base)	2001	2006	2011	2016	2021
Under 15	9,444	9,435	9,106	8,827	8,715	8,750
15 - 44	20,738	20,868	20,771	20,074	19,467	19,368
45 - 59	8,856	9,406	10,009	10,621	11,305	10,987
60 - 74	6,509	6,448	6,849	7,771	8,282	8,861
75 and over	3,542	3,714	3,792	3,869	4,062	4,518
Total	49,089	49,871	50,526	51,161	51,832	52,484

Note: Detail does not always add to total owing to rounding

Source: Government Actuary's Department

Over the period that the household projections cover, 1996 to 2021, the population of England is projected to rise by 3.4 million, or 6.9 per cent. The population aged 15 and over is, however, projected to rise distinctly faster, both absolutely and in proportional terms, by 4.1 million or 10.3 per cent. The increase is distributed very unevenly by age groups as a consequence of the variability of the number of births per year far back in the past, particularly the rise in births from 1941 and especially immediately after the war; the so called "baby boom" from 1956 which peaked in the mid 1960s and then the fall in births to the mid 1970s. As an introduction to the assumptions about the three components of population change: births, deaths and migration, Table C.2 shows their contribution to the projected increase in the total population. They are expressed in annual averages for five year periods.

Table C.2 Projected Components of Change of the Population in England 1996 - 2021 (annual averages in thousands)					
	1996 - 2001	2001 - 6	2006 - 11	2011 - 16	2016 - 21
Births	607	585	575	583	591
less Deaths	525	520	514	515	526
Natural increase	**81**	**65**	**61**	**68**	**64**
Migration	75	66	66	66	66
Total increase	**156**	**131**	**127**	**134**	**130**

Source: C Shaw, "1996-based National Population Projections", *Population Trends*, No 91 (March 1998) Table 3

About one half of the projected net increase in the total population is the direct result of net inward migration, excluding the additional births due to net migration raising the number of women of child bearing age in the population. The full effect of migration on the projected population, including the additional births net of deaths of inward migrants, may be shown by comparing the main projection for 2021 analysed by age (Table C.3) with a "natural change" projection for the same year. A "natural change" projection includes only births to members of the base (i.e. 1996) population and their children and deaths among the base population.

Table C.3: Projections of the Population of England in 2021 (thousands)			
	2021		
Age	Main projection	Natural change	Difference
Under 15	8,750	8,123	-627
15 - 44	19,368	17,972	-1,396
45 - 59	10,987	10,638	-349
60 - 74	8,861	8,822	-39
75 and over	4,518	4,529	+11
Total	**52,484**	**50,084**	**-2,400**

Migrants are predominantly young adults (see Table C.9 below), hence the high proportion of the difference between the main (with migration) projection and the natural increase projection, that is in the 15-44 age range. Most, but not all, of the difference in the under 15 age group is due to children born to migrants. That the natural change projection is higher for the 75 and over age group is due to outward exceeding inward migration at ages 65 and over. The assumptions about future migration are discussed later in this Annex.

Births

Births after the 1996 base date cannot affect the population aged 15 and over until after 2011 and the population aged 20 and over not until after 2016. In the more distant years of the projection, however, the effect of the assumption about future births on the projected number of households is not negligible. In the longer term, changes in assumptions about future births can have large effects on the size of the population and hence the household projections.

Assumptions about future births are complex; but may be summarised in terms of the average completed family size (i.e. live births per woman) which GAD currently assume in the longer term will be 1.80. This is some 14 per cent below the replacement level of 2.1. The significance of the fertility assumption for the projected population of household forming age may be gauged by comparing the projected population aged 15-19 in 2016 and aged 15-19 and 20-24 in 2021 in the main projection with the GAD's low fertility variant which assumes a long term family size of 1.60, see Table C.4. The variant projections are made for the United Kingdom, so the comparison with the main projection must be in UK terms. But since in the main projection England accounts for 84 per cent of all UK births in 1996 - 2021, the UK comparison gives a fair picture for England as well.

Table C.4: Impact of Fertility Assumptions on Projected Population of Household Forming Age (thousands)			
	Difference Between Principal and Low Fertility Projections		
Population Aged	2011	2016	2021
15 - 19	nil	166	397
20 - 24	nil	nil	166
25 - 29	nil	nil	nil
Source: Government Actuary's Department			

Deaths

In contrast to fertility, the assumptions about mortality have an immediate effect on the projected population of household forming age. At most ages, mortality rates have been falling for many years. Hence in deciding on assumptions for projecting the population, the question is how fast and how far this fall will continue. Mortality assumptions are complex; for a full account reference should be made to *National population projections 1996-based*, PP2 No 21. The implications of the specific assumptions are summarised in two ways in Table C.5. expectation of life at birth and standardised death rates. The standardised death rate is the death rate (that is the total number of deaths divided by total population) resulting from applying death rates for a particular year to the population number for a standard year, taken here as the year 1991. The ratios of these rates for selected years to that for a standard year (actually the average of three years 1990 - 92 in this case) is given in Table C.5. Expectations of life and standardised death rates are shown separately for males and females. Female life expectancy is higher than for males, but since around 1980, life expectancy has risen faster for males. This trend is projected to continue. It is important for household projections, because it means that married couple households continue to higher ages and widowhood begins later. This effect is discussed further in Annex D on marital status.

Table C.5 Expectation of Life at Birth and Standardised Death Rates (United Kingdom)				
	Expectation of life at birth (years)		Standardised Death Rates (1990 - 92 = 1.00)	
	Male	Female	Male	Female
1981	70.9	76.9	1.20	1.17
1986	71.9	77.7	1.12	1.10
1991	73.2	78.7	1.01	1.01
1996	74.4	79.5	0.92	0.94
2001	75.3	80.2	0.85	0.90
2011	76.9	81.5	0.73	0.80
2021	77.9	82.6	0.67	0.72
Source: *National population projections 1996 based* (Series PP2 No 21) Table 8.3				

The standardised death rates in Table C.5 fell by 23 per cent for men and 20 per cent for women between 1981 and 1996 and further reductions are projected between 1996 and 2021 of 27 per cent for men and 23 per cent for women. The basis for the projected fall in death rates is explained in Chapter 8 of *National population projections 1996-based*.

The mortality assumption affects primarily the population at the higher ages. The Government Actuary's Department's higher variant mortality assumption (see Annex G) results in a projected population in 2021 345,000 lower than the principal projection. 85 per cent of the difference is in the population aged 60 or over; 60 per cent is in the population aged 75 or over.

The importance of falling mortality for the projected increase in the population can be shown by comparison with what would happen if mortality were to remain constant at the base year level. This is, of course, a purely hypothetical calculation for purposes of exposition. In comparison with the main projection (Tables C.1 and C.2) deaths would run 53,000 a year higher in 2006 - 11 and 74,000 a year in 2016 - 21. Without the projected fall in mortality, the projected population in 2021 would be some 1.2 million lower. All but 35,000 of the difference would be at age 15 and over. Fuller detail is in Table C.6.

Table C.6: Comparison of the Main Population Projection for 2011 and 2021 with Constant Mortality Projection (thousands)

Age	2011			2021		
	Main projection	Constant mortality	Difference	Main projection	Constant mortality	Difference
Under 15	8,827	8,809	18	8,750	8,715	35
15 - 44	20,074	20,068	6	19,368	19,343	25
45 - 59	10,621	10,590	31	10,987	10,925	62
60 - 74	7,771	7,589	182	8,861	8,491	370
75 and over	3,869	3,607	262	4,518	3,803	715
Total	51,161	50,664	497	52,484	51,278	1,206

Below age 60 the effect of mortality on the population projections is small. But from 60 onwards and especially above 75, the effect is strong.

Migration

Table C.7: Net Migration Flows: England (thousands)

		Net civilian migration				Other changes	
	Natural change	Within UK	Irish Republic	Beyond British Isles	Total	(*)	Total
1971-76 (Annual average)	75	+1	-9	-27	-35	+10	+50
1976-81 (Annual average)	31	+6	-3	-15	-11	+12	+32
1981-86 (Annual average)	56	+7	+4	+28	+39	+12	+107
1986-7	108	+8	+5	+42	+55	-19	+145
1987-8	115	+6	+20	+2	+28	+2	+146
1988-89	120	-5	+22	+45	+62	-7	+175
1989-90	106	-13	+14	+67	+68	+9	+183
1990 - 1	133	-20	-	+107	+88	-4	+216
1991 - 2	133	-15	-6	+60	+40	-2	+170
1992 - 3	114	-11	-2	+45	+32	+8	+154
1993 - 4	100	-8	+1	+67	+59	+15	+175
1994 - 5	96	-	+1	+99	+100	-	+196
1995 - 6	72	+1	-1	+104	+104	+9	+186
1996 - 7	92	+4	-5	+97	+96	+8	+195

(*) Mainly movements of personnel of HM Forces and US Forces

Source: *Population Trends* No 94 Table 5 and Table 1.2 of *International migration* Series MN 19, 20, 21, 22 and 23

Within the time horizon of the household projections, net migration is the most uncertain of the components of change of the adult population. The contribution of net inward migration to the projected growth of the population of England between 1996 and 2021 was shown in Table C.2. The basis for projecting net inward migration on the scale assumed is the past course of migration. This is summarised in aggregate in Table C.7, which shows the contribution of the net migration flows to the net change in the population of England.

The swing from near continuous net outward migration to beyond the British Isles in the 1970s and early 1980s to net inward migration, shown in Table C.7, lay behind a continuation of net inward migration being assumed in the 1991-based projections. A new methodology for the migration assumptions was developed (see "National Population Projections: a new methodology for determining migration assumptions", *Occasional Paper 42*, OPCS 1993). It was first used in the 1991-based projections and was used also in the 1992- and 1994-based population projections. It has been used, with minor modifications, in the present 1996-based projections. Further detail about trends in international migration is in L Vickers, "Trends in Migration in the UK", *Population Trends*, No 94 (1998).

International migration assumptions are specified in the first instance for the United Kingdom and then subsequently apportioned among the component countries. Separate assumptions are made about inward and outward movement of British citizens and other nationals, by category of origin and destination. The International Passenger Survey (IPS) is the main source of data on international migration. However it needs to be supplemented with information from the Home Office on asylum seekers and other visitor switchers and estimates of migration between the UK and the Irish Republic since these two types of flows are excluded from the IPS. Only combining all three will give a true picture of migration. The assumptions for the medium and long term are summarised in Table C.8.

Table C.8: Assumptions About International Migration: United Kingdom 1998 - 99 Onwards (thousands per year)			
British Citizens	**In**	**Out**	**Net**
Old Commonwealth, S Africa, USA	40	45	-5
New Commonwealth	20	15	5
European Economic Area	45	45	0
Other countries	10	10	0
Not British Citizens			
Old Commonwealth, S Africa, USA	45	35	10
New Commonwealth	30	15	15
European Economic Area	40	25	15
Other countries	40	25	15
Irish Republic	15	15	0
Visitor Switchers (a)	25	5	20
Total civilian migration (b)	**305**	**240**	**65**

Note: (a) Persons admitted as short term visitors who are subsequently granted an extension of stay, for instance, on marriage; also includes asylum seekers whose applications are accepted

(b) Includes 5,000 taken off the inflow and 5,000 added to the outflow to partially down weight the very high net inflows in the latest two years

Source: *National Population Projections 1996-based* PP2 No 21, Table 9.1

For England net inward migration from outside the United Kingdom is assumed to be 65,500 a year from 1988 - 99 and net inward migration from Scotland, Wales and Northern Ireland (combined) 500 a year. These sum to the net inflow of 66,000 a year shown in Table C.2. In 1996 - 97 and 1997 - 98 net inward migration to England was assumed to be 96,000 and 81,500 respectively.

Inward and outward migrants are predominantly young. The age structure of the 65,000 a year of net migration to the United Kingdom is shown in Table C.9. Women aged 15 - 44 are shown separately owing to migration of women of child bearing age being important for consequential effects on births.

Table C.9	Age Structure of Net Inward Migration to the United Kingdom (thousands)
Under 15	6.3
15 - 44 male	25.6
15 - 44 female	30.6
45 - 64	2.9
65 and over	-0.5
All ages	**65.0**

Differences from the 1992-based population projection

How the present 1996-based population projection differs from the 1992-based projection from which the 1992-based household projections were derived may be shown by comparing the projected population changes between 1996 and 2021. For the 1996-based projections, population changes from 1992 to 1996 are outturn. 2021 was beyond the time horizon of the 1992-based household projections. But since the 1996-based household projections extend to 2021, the population projections are compared over that period. The older population is analysed in finer detail because there are important differences between the 1996-based and 1992-based household projections at the high ages. The difference between projected male and female mortality (Table C.5) is important at these ages.

The projected increase in the population aged 15 and over during the quarter century is almost 300,000 higher in the 1996-based projection than in the 1992-based projection. The increase in the population aged 25 and over, among which the proportion of men and women heading households is higher than in the 15 - 24 group, is nearly 450 thousand higher in the 1996-based projection, owing to the effect of the higher inward migration that is assumed.

Table C.10: Projected Changes in the Population of England 1996 - 2021 (thousands)		
Age	**1992-based projection**	**1996-based projection**
Under 15	-556	-694
15 - 24	+217	+72
25 - 44	-1,730	-1,441
45 - 59	+1,955	+2,130
60 - 74	+2,312	+2,352
75 - 84		
Male	+423	+435
Female	+182	+220
Total	**+605**	**+655**
85 and over		
Male	+230	+184
Female	+208	+137
Total	**+438**	**+321**
All ages	**+3,240**	**+3,395**

Source: *National population projections 1992-based* PP2 No 19 Appendix 1(d) and *1996-based* PP2 No 21 Appendix 1(d)

Differences between the projected net increases in the population in the 1992-based and 1996-based projections are (by definition) the outcome of differences in the assumptions about future births, deaths and migration, together with differences in the 1996-base due to the figures for that year being a projection in the 1992-based projection, but outturn for the 1996-based projection. The assumptions are compared in tabular form in Table C.11.

Table C.11: Projection Assumptions for England (1992-based and 1996-based Compared)		
	1992-based projection	**1996-based projection**
Fertility Average number of children per woman for women born after 1980	1.90	1.80
Mortality Expectation of life at birth in 2021 (years)		
Males	77.8	78.1
Females	82.8	82.7
Migration Annual net flow from 1998 - 99	+58,000(a)	+66,000
Note:(a) This annual rate was assumed to continue to 2006 - 07 then tapered down to zero in 2016 - 17		
Source: *Government Actuary's Department*		

The contribution of these differences in assumptions, together with differences in the 1996 figures, to the difference in the population projections for 2021, is shown in Table C.12 for the population aged 16 and over.

Table C.12: Analysis of Differences Between the 1992-Based and 1996-Based Projections of the Population Aged 16 and Over In 2021 (thousands)			
	1992-based	**1996-based**	**Difference**
Population at 1996 aged 16 and over	38,934	39,036	+103
plus Population aged 0 - 15 in 1996	10,133	10,053	-80
plus Births in 1996 - 2005	5,673	5,380	-293
plus Net migration	862	1,649	+787
less Deaths	12,856	12,965	+108
Population at 2021 aged 16 and over	42,745	43,153	+408
Source: Government Actuary's Department			

The starting population in 1996 was 103,000 higher than in the 1992-based projection owing to net inward migration having run higher than expected. On top of this, the projected increase in the population aged 16 and over between 1996 and 2021 is 305,000 higher in the 1996-based projections. This gives a total population at 2021 that is 408,000 higher. The higher increase between 1996 and 2021 is the net outcome of a downward effect of 80 thousand fewer children at 1996, 293,000 fewer births, an upward effect of 787,000 from net migration and a downward effect of 108,000 from more deaths. The importance of the assumption about migration stands out. The increase in projected deaths is due to deaths at the high ages, where a somewhat slower fall in death rates is assumed in the 1996-based projections (see also Table C.10). Note that the 1992-based household projections only went to 2016. At 2016 the net migration effect is smaller.

ANNEX D
Projections of marital status

Marital status is here used to comprise both legal marital status and unmarried cohabitation. Projections were first made of legal marital status and then within each category of legal marital status, the proportion cohabiting. This sequence is made necessary by the limited data available about cohabitation, which are of the proportions of members of population groups defined by sex, legal marital status and by age. As is described in more detail later in this Annex, past trends in the proportions cohabiting in population groups defined by sex, legal marital status and age are the basis for projecting the number of cohabiting men and women in future. These trends in cohabitation are closely related to the trends in marriage rates which are a very important element in the projections of legal marital status. The rising trend in cohabitation by never married men and women is doubtless one of the main reasons for the declining trend in first marriage rates, on which the assumptions about future marriage rates were based. That the assumptions about marriage rates and cohabitation were consistent one with another was checked by examining changes in projected proportions married and cohabiting combined over the projection period.

The 1996-based projections of legal marital status are described first, then the 1996-based projections of cohabitation and then what these projections imply about the proportions of men and women living in couple partnerships. Differences from the previous 1992-based projections of marital status and cohabitation are then discussed.

Projection of legal marital status

The Government Actuary's Department has prepared new projections of the legal marital status of the population of England and Wales. Details of the methodology and the full results are published in C Shaw "1996-based population projections by legal marital status for England and Wales", *Population Trends No 95* (Spring 1999). These projections were made by a "component" methodology, in which assumptions are made about future values for each of the components of change, that is first marriage rates, remarriage rates, divorce rates, death rates by marital status and migration by marital status. Assumptions about each are determined from past trends. These are analysed separately by age group: marriage rates and divorce rates vary with age. These age specific rates for past years and the marital status specific death rates relate to England and Wales, because population estimates by marital status are available only at this level. Therefore the marital status projections presented in this Annex are for England and Wales also. For purposes of household projections, marital status estimates for England are derived. In nearly all categories of age and sex, the population of England is between 94 and 95 per cent of the population of England and Wales combined. There is little scope for the marital status of the population of England to differ materially from that of England and Wales. The projections of the marital status of the population of England and Wales can therefore be taken for present purposes as applying in proportional terms to England.

The detail of the assumptions about marriage and divorce rates is too complex to summarise fully here. But in broad terms a continuation of the past fall in first marriage rates at ages under 30 is assumed up to 2006, with a partially offsetting increase at ages above 30 on the hypothesis that part of the fall in marriage rates at the younger ages reflects marriages being deferred until later in life. A modest further increase in age specific divorce rates is assumed. Divorce rates have been fairly steady since 1993, but this was considered too short a period to show that the long rise in divorce rates is at an end, or even being reversed. Table D.1 shows the projected marriage and divorce rates and the number of marriages and divorces, together with corresponding figures for earlier years. The marital status projection model operates at an individual rather than a couple level. Therefore the projected future number of marriages can be analysed by the previous marital status of each member individually, but not in combination. So, for example, the total number of bachelors marrying spinsters is not available. The division between first marriages and remarriages for men and women is not identical but is fairly similar. The table therefore divides marriages into first marriages and remarriages for the bridegroom, together with the first marriage rate for men.

Table D.1: Marriages and Divorces in England and Wales, Projections to 2021						
	Marriages by Men			**Divorces**		
	First marriages ('000)	**Remarriages ('000)**	**Total ('000)**	**First marriage rate (a)**	**Number ('000)**	**Divorce rate (b)**
1981	259	93	352	51.7	146	11.9
1986	253	95	348	44.5	154	12.9
1991	223	84	307	37.0	159	13.5
1993	213	86	299	34.7	165	14.2
1996	193	86	279	29.8	157	13.9
2001	194	80	274	27.2	141	12.9
2006	206	77	283	26.3	128	12.1
2011	220	76	296	26.0	118	11.3
2016	230	73	303	25.7	112	10.9
2021	232	71	303	25.0	109	10.7

Notes: (a) Per 1,000 single males aged 16 and over

(b) Per 1,000 married men aged 16 and over

Source: Office of National Statistics and Government Actuary's Department

First marriage rates and divorce rates are shown in a highly aggregated way in Table D.1. First marriage rates specific for age level off around 2006, although age specific divorce rates are assumed to rise only modestly. The table shows the overall divorce rate which falls, reflecting the changing age structure of the married population. An increasing proportion are at the ages where divorce rates are low. Implications of the marriage and divorce assumptions may also be shown in terms of the proportion of men and women ever marrying and the proportion of first marriages ended by divorce.

Table D.2: Projected Proportions of Men and Women Ever Marrying and Proportions of First Marriages Ended by Divorce (per cent)						
	Men			**Women**		
	1980 - 82	**1995 - 96**	**2011 - 12**	**1980 - 82**	**1995 - 96**	**2011 - 12**
Proportion ever marrying	84	67	66	89	73	71
Proportion of divorced men and women remarrying	83	62	56	74	57	51
Proportion of first marriages ended by divorce	n.a.	39	38	n.a.	38	38

Note: These are life table calculations that show the proportion that would ever marry or divorce if people were to experience the age specific marriage or divorce rates of the year in question throughout their adult life.

Source: Shaw (1999) Table 2

The continuing momentum of past changes in marriage and divorce rates that is as their effects spread to older age groups, rather than the assumed further changes in marriage and divorce rates, is the main reason for the projected future changes in the legal marital status of the population. The marital status proportions that are projected are shown in Table D.3. For reasons of space only the projections for 2011 and 2021 are shown.

Table D.3: Projected Marital Status Proportions 1996 to 2021 (proportions per thousand population)

	Men				Women			
	Single	Married	Divorced	Widowed	Single	Married	Divorced	Widowed
Aged 20 - 29								
1996	785	197	18	0	652	313	34	1
2011	879	112	8	0	793	189	18	0
2021	874	117	9	0	786	195	19	0
Aged 30 - 44								
1996	261	622	115	3	173	689	132	6
2011	454	451	92	2	355	523	118	4
2021	499	421	78	2	412	486	99	3
Aged 45 - 59								
1996	90	772	123	14	52	765	135	48
2011	179	630	179	11	121	657	191	31
2021	279	553	158	10	210	587	176	26
Aged 60 - 74								
1996	76	781	61	83	60	597	68	276
2011	78	732	132	59	48	620	148	184
2021	115	670	163	52	76	582	184	157
Aged 75 and over								
1996	64	625	26	286	88	237	26	650
2011	64	628	60	248	55	293	61	591
2021	64	620	99	217	44	335	106	516

Note: Proportions do not always sum to 1,000 owing to rounding

Source: Calculated from tables supplied by the Government Actuary's Department

The most marked changes shown between 1996 and 2021 in the marital status distribution are the rise in the proportion of men and women in the 20-29 and 30-44 age groups who are single (in the sense of never married) and the decline in the proportion of women and to a lesser extent men, who are widows (or widowers). The marital status distribution is strongly influenced by ageing. The rise in the proportions of divorced men and women in the 60-74 and 75 and over age groups, for instance, is due not to more couples in those age ranges divorcing, but to men and women who had divorced in earlier years growing older.

Table D.4: Projection of the Population of England and Wales Aged 16 and Over Analysed by Legal Marital Status (thousands)

	1996	2001	2006	2011	2016	2021
Males						
Single	6,482	7,130	7,838	8,465	8,924	9,283
Married	11,339	10,927	10,598	10,407	10,301	10,211
Divorced	1,543	1,824	2,038	2,178	2,266	2,318
Widowed	728	716	708	709	716	731
Total	20,091	20,597	21,182	21,759	22,207	22,543
Females						
Single	5,171	5,750	6,397	6,966	7,372	7,697
Married	11,406	10,987	10,658	10,466	10,359	10,267
Divorced	1,819	2,113	2,349	2,527	2,662	2,762
Widowed	2,870	2,718	2,570	2,455	2,390	2,380
Total	21,265	21,568	21,974	22,413	22,783	23,106

Source: Government Actuary's Department

The large fall in the proportion of women aged 60-74 and 75 and over who are widows is mainly the consequence of lower death rates of older men. Women are widowed later in life, with an effect on the number of widows that is not fully compensated for by widows at any given age living longer. The fall in female death rates at the high ages similarly is the main reason for the fall in the proportion of widowers.

The projected population analysed by marital status is shown in Table D.4. It refers to England and Wales, hence the differences from Table C.1 in Annex C.

A fall of 1.1 million (each) in the number of married men and women is projected between 1996 and 2021 and an increase of 1.7 million persons in the divorced population. Excluding males and females under age 20 among whom both marriage rates and cohabitation rates are low, there are projected increases in the single population of 2.76 million men and 2.48 million women. An analysis by age of the never married population is shown in Table D.5, as for single men and women the propensity to live alone rises with age. For space reasons figures are shown for 1996, 2001, 2011 and 2021. The 16-19 age group is omitted as the proportion that live independently is low.

Table D.5 Analysis by Age of the Projected Never Married Population (thousands)				
	1996	2001	2011	2021
Men				
20 - 24	1,597	1,547	1,745	1,626
25 - 34	2,223	2,353	2,384	2,547
35 - 44	657	1,051	1,503	1,516
45 - 54	323	394	830	1,195
55 - 64	189	211	337	716
65 - 74	158	145	161	266
75 and over	84	94	104	127
Total over 20	**5,231**	**5,795**	**7,064**	**7,992**
Women				
20 - 24	1,369	1,388	1,586	1,475
25 - 34	1,537	1,741	1,952	2,101
35 - 44	414	684	1,087	1,218
45 - 54	183	238	554	883
55 - 64	128	130	212	492
65 - 74	154	125	112	186
75 and over	216	188	138	124
Total over 20	**4,000**	**4,493**	**5,642**	**6,479**

Source: Government Actuary's Department

Noteworthy is how many of the projected increase in the number of never married men and women are in the 35-64 age range, not the younger ages under 35. In the twenty five year projection period, just over 80 per cent of the projected net increase in never married men is in the 35-64 range; one half are middle aged (45-64). For women, the proportions are 75 per cent aged 35-64 and 43 per cent aged 45-64. How this prospect is modified by taking account of cohabitation is considered in the next section of the Annex.

Cohabitation

For projections of the number of households, an extremely important question is how much of the projected increase in the number of never married men and women will be offset by more unmarried cohabitation. Projections of the number of cohabiting men and women, analysed by their legal marital status are published in C Shaw and J Haskey, "New estimates and projections of the population cohabiting in England and Wales", *Population Trends No 95*, Spring 1999. This article describes the sources and methods used for the base estimate of cohabiting men and women analysed by age and legal marital status and for the projections. The projection method for cohabitation is different from that for legal marital status. For legal marital status, flows into and out of the marital statuses year by year are projected. Data about cohabitation are not sufficiently detailed for the same method to be used for projecting the cohabiting population.

Projections of cohabitation have therefore to be made by projecting proportions of the population cohabiting, specific for sex, age and marital status. The proportions are projected from trends over time as discerned from the General Household Survey (GHS). Data on cohabitation by males was first collected by GHS in 1986, so data are available from 1986 to 1996. Owing to the sample size available, there are erratic variations from year to year, which lead to a degree of uncertainty about the pace of any trends. For the 1996-based projections, the proportions of formerly married (mainly divorced but also including separated and widowed) people who are cohabiting are assumed to remain at 1996 levels, specific for age and sex. Among never married men and women, a further increase is projected. The steep rise in cohabitation at the younger ages is still a fairly recent phenomenon. If they continue to cohabit as they grow older, then the higher proportions cohabiting at the younger age will feed through to successively higher ages. This would be expected as attitudes to cohabitation change, in particular as it moves from being seen as a prelude to marriage to being accepted as an alternative to marriage. The 1996-based projection of cohabitation is summarised in Table D.6. In the projection the number of cohabiting men and women are equal. Since by convention the male partner is taken to be household head or representative, the table shows cohabiting men analysed by age and legal marital status. "Formerly married" includes legally married but separated.

Table D.6: 1996-Based Projection of Cohabiting Men: England and Wales (thousands)				
	1996	**2001**	**2011**	**2021**
Aged under 25				
Never married	222	238	296	279
Formerly married	2	1	2	2
Total	**225**	**240**	**298**	**281**
Aged 25 - 34				
Never married	608	724	803	871
Formerly married	120	85	53	58
Total	**728**	**809**	**856**	**929**
Aged 35 - 44				
Never married	148	316	550	560
Formerly married	190	218	165	128
Total	**338**	**534**	**715**	**688**
Aged 45 - 54				
Never married	35	86	265	379
Formerly married	147	173	220	170
Total	**182**	**259**	**485**	**549**
Aged 55 and over				
Never married	11	54	129	256
Formerly married	77	104	171	224
Total	**87**	**158**	**300**	**480**
All ages				
Never married	1,025	1,419	2,043	2,345
Formerly married	535	581	611	582
Total	**1,560**	**2,001**	**2,654**	**2,926**

Source: Table 3 in C Shaw and J Haskey, "New Estimates and Projections of the Population Cohabiting in England and Wales", *Population Trends* No 95 (1999)

The projected increase in cohabitation is concentrated among the never married. The assumed increase in proportions cohabiting interacts with the projected large rise in the number of legally never married men and women (Table D.5) to produce an increase of nearly 1.4 million in the number of cohabiting couples in the projection period. Most of the projected increase is at ages 35 and over. In 1996, 80 per cent of never married cohabiting men (and 88 per cent of women) were under age 35; but of the projected increase between 1996 and 2021, over 70 per cent, is at ages 35 and over. What is being projected is in effect that cohabiting couples continue in that status as they age, instead of becoming legally married. The increase of nearly a quarter of a million never married cohabiting couples aged 55 and over is almost certainly to be interpreted in terms of ageing and not of older men and women beginning cohabitations.

Married and cohabiting couples and never married non-cohabiting men and women

To see the prospect for future numbers of couple households and also what the projected increase in the total never married population and in never married cohabiters implies for the number of single men and women likely to live alone, the projections by legal marital status (Tables D.4 and D.5) and cohabitation (Table D.6) are brought together. The changing proportion of men living in partnerships (i.e. married or cohabiting) is shown in Table D.7. Married men who are separated and cohabiting are included with cohabiting to avoid double counting. In the table, living in partnerships includes all cohabiters, not just never married, as a proportion of the whole male population.

Table D.7: Proportions of Men Married or Cohabiting						
	Age					
	16 - 24	25 - 34	35 - 44	45 - 54	55 - 64	65 and over
1996						
Number ('000)	331	2,502	2,769	2,735	2,063	2,430
Per cent	11.2	58.7	76.9	81.0	82.1	72.0
2001						
Number ('000)	310	2,090	3,006	2,737	2,211	2,513
Per cent	10.4	54.6	72.9	78.5	80.9	72.4
2011						
Number ('000)	372	1,754	2,608	2,942	2,516	2,814
Per cent	11.5	51.6	67.7	72.4	76.5	71.6
2021						
Number ('000)	351	1,908	2,256	2,553	2,724	3,296
Per cent	11.7	52.2	65.8	67.1	70.4	68.7
Source: Calculated from Table 5 of C Shaw and J Haskey (1999)						

The projected increase in cohabitation only partially offsets the reduction in marriage rates. In consequence, a large increase in the number of non-cohabiting men and women not in couples, i.e. neither married nor cohabiting, is projected. The changes are summarised in Table D.8. Figures are shown for the 20-24 age group rather than 16-24 because so few of the 16-19 group live independently.

The projected increase in the number of never married non-cohabiting men and women is primarily at ages 35 and over. Among men all but 40,000 of the projected net increase of just under 1,450,000 in the number of never married non-cohabiting men aged 20 and over in the projection period from 1996 to 2021 are shown in Table D.8 as aged 35 and over and 960,000 are aged 45 and over. Among never married non-cohabiting women aged 20 and over just over 250,000 of the projected increase is at age under 35 and 835,000 at age 35 and over. The increase in non-cohabiting never married men and women, especially men, will thus be middle aged and not young.

Among formerly married men who are not cohabiting, a large increase, over 800,000, is projected over the 25 years at aged 55 and over. This is principally the result of divorced men growing older rather than more widowers. Among women also the increase in the number aged 55 and over who are not cohabiting comes from ageing of divorced women, not more widows.

Table D.8: Projections of Men and Women not in couples (thousands)

	20 - 24	25 - 34	35 - 44	45 - 54	55 - 64	65 - 74	75 and over
Men							
1996							
Never married	1,412	1,615	509	287	182	155	83
Formerly married	3	147	324	356	267	304	402
2001							
Never married	1,350	1,629	735	308	177	129	90
Formerly married	2	107	382	442	346	305	436
2011							
Never married	1,495	1,581	953	565	247	130	96
Formerly married	2	62	291	557	527	405	487
2021							
Never married	1,390	1,676	956	816	521	214	117
Formerly married	2	68	218	435	624	564	608
Women							
1996							
Never married	1,060	991	309	164	124	152	215
Formerly married	6	216	405	481	535	938	1,651
2001							
Never married	1,053	1,049	436	175	104	109	181
Formerly married	3	171	467	558	601	859	1,684
2011							
Never married	1,182	1,122	602	333	140	108	130
Formerly married	4	109	385	667	795	916	1,625
2021							
Never married	1,099	1,209	678	536	324	143	116
Formerly married	3	118	290	542	878	1,120	1,752

Source: As Table D.7, with additional detail from the Government Actuary's Department

Comparison with the previous (1992-based) projections of marital status

In Annex D of *Projections of Households in England to 2016*, the 1992-based projections of marital status were given only to 2011. A comparison is therefore made between the 1996-based projections for 2011 and the 1992-based projections for 2011. The projections shown in *Projections of Household in England to 2016* (Table D.4) were of the marital status of the population aged 15 and over, so the 1996 projection must be on the same basis, hence the differences from Table D.4 above.

Table D.9: Projections of the Population of England and Wales by Marital Status in 2011: 1992-Based and 1996-Based (thousands)

	1992-based	1996-based	Difference
Males			
Single (15 and over)	7,714	8,796	+1,082
Married	11,218	10,407	-811
Divorced	2,370	2,178	-193
Widowed	746	709	-37
Total	**22,048**	**22,089**	**+41**
Females			
Single (15 and over)	5,768	7,278	+1,510
Married	11,255	10,466	-789
Divorced	2,702	2,527	-176
Widowed	2,948	2,455	-493
Total	**22,673**	**22,725**	**+53**

The much higher projected totals of single men and women (especially women) stand out, as do the lower projected totals of married men and women. The reduction in the projected number of widows is also important for household projections. The differences between the 1992-based and 1996-based projections can be attributed to:

(i)   revisions to the base population estimates of marital status;

(ii)   marriage and divorce rates and other new information since 1992; and

(iii)   a new and improved projection methodology.

For the 1992-based projection the base was marital status estimates "rolled forward" from the 1981 Census. Since then the Office for National Statistics produced new estimates based on the 1991 Census (*Population Trends No 89* (1997)), which differed from the previous estimates. In addition first marriage rates at young ages fell faster after 1992, which contributes to the lower number of married men and women. The new methodology for projecting marital status is described in Shaw (1999). It takes advantage of recent advances in computer software for dealing with complex multi-dimensional projections. It is superior to the previous method in that it depends on explicit assumptions about marriage, remarriage and divorce rates, on deaths by marital status and the marital status of migrants instead of projecting net changes. The previous method can be seen not to have dealt adequately with the ageing on effects of the fall in first marriage rates at young ages, nor the degree to which improvements in male mortality would affect the future number of widows.

Table D.10: Projections of Cohabiting Men and Women in 2011 (thousands)			
	1992-based projection	**1996-based projection**	**Difference**
Men			
Never married	914	2,043	+1,129
Formerly married	720	611	-109
Total	**1,635**	**2,654**	**+1,019**
Women			
Never married	1,003	2,147	+1,144
Formerly married	632	507	-125
Total	**1,635**	**2,654**	**+1,019**

Source: Table D.5 above and Table D8 of *Projections of Households in England to 2016*

There are large differences as well in the 1992-based and 1996-based projections of cohabitation. As Table D.10 shows, the differences are almost entirely in the projected numbers of never married cohabiting men and women and are the consequence of the increase in the projected number of never married men and women (Table D.8) and the assumption of further increases in the proportion of cohabiters among never married men and women in each age group. In the 1992-based projections, in contrast, these proportions were assumed to remain constant.

ANNEX E
Projections of the institutional population

A comprehensive count of the institutional population, that is to say persons whose usual residence is what is called in census terminology a "communal establishment", is available only from the Census. At the younger and middle ages the institutional population lives in a multiplicity of different categories of communal establishment. Post 1991 information about the number of people in some types of establishment is very incomplete, without the detail required to estimate how many are usually resident there. It was therefore considered not possible to make an estimate of the institutional population under age 65 for a year or years since 1991 to compare with the 1992-based projection. The same assumption has therefore to be made for the 1996-based projection, that the institutional population throughout the projection period will remain the same as in 1991 in numerical terms, in each population category defined by sex, age and legal marital status.

At the higher ages, the diversity of types of communal establishment is less. At ages above 75, residential care homes and nursing homes are dominant. The 1991 Census (*Communal Establishments*, Table 3) recorded 89 per cent of all residents aged 75-84 of communal establishments in England as being residents of residential care homes and nursing homes. In the 85 and over age group, the proportion was 93 per cent. In the 65-74 age group the proportion of residents of communal establishments that lived in residential care homes was lower at 74 per cent, with 16 per cent resident in hospital (as compared with 9 per cent of those aged 75-84 and 6 per cent at age 85 and over). Information about the number of residents in residential care homes and nursing homes could therefore be used as the basis for a fairly secure estimate of the institutional population aged 75 and over. It could also provide a pointer to changes in the institutional population aged 65-74. The information about the number of men and women living in residential care and nursing homes since 1991 is summarised in the next section of this Annex.

Department of Health information about residential care and nursing home residents, year by year

The Department of Health (DH) collects information from residential care homes and nursing homes through annual returns made by registered homes. Registration is compulsory under statute. For **residential care homes** the information available from 1991 onwards includes for each year the number of residents divided into long stay and short stay, each divided by age into under 65, 65-74, 75-84 and 85 and over. Separate figures are not collected for men and women, nor is there any analysis by marital status. At the time of writing, this information is available for 1991 to 1996 (at the end of March).

The number of long stay residents in residential care homes according to returns to the Department of Health are shown in Table E.1. Short stay residents are excluded as they are less likely to have been counted as "resident" in the Census.

Table E.1: Long Stay Residents in Residential Care Homes (in thousands at end March)			
	Age 65 - 74	Age 75 - 84	Age 85 and over	Total aged 65 and over
1991	26.9	91.9	115.7	234.5
1992	26.2	88.1	117.3	231.6
1993	26.2	83.7	119.1	229.0
1994	26.2	81.2	122.4	229.8
1995	25.3	79.3	124.5	229.1
1996	26.1	78.7	126.6	231.4
Source: Department of Health			

For **nursing homes** similar information has been collected since 1993/94, that is the number of residents (the term in the DH tables is "occupied beds") at the end of March in each year. It is available for 1994 to 1997. Before 1993/94 the return collected only the number of beds, not the number of residents. The number of registered beds from 1991 and the number of occupied beds from 1994 are shown in Table E.2. The registered beds are described as "registered beds for the elderly"; so the number of them occupied by persons under 65 may be assumed to be negligible (the published age analysis for nursing homes - unlike residential care homes - distinguishes only 65-74, 75-84 and 85 and over. As with residential care homes, no analysis by sex or marital status is available.

Table E.2: Registered Beds and "Occupied Beds" in Nursing Homes (thousands at end of March)					
	"Occupied Beds"				Total Registered
	65 - 74	**75 - 84**	**85 and over**	**Total**	**Beds**
1991	...	...	...	...	109.0
1992	...	...	...	...	124.0
1993	...	...	...	...	144.3
1994	19.1	51.4	61.7	132.4	149.5
1995	19.9	51.1	64.5	135.5	155.4
1996	18.6	50.1	64.7	133.4	159.2
1997	18.0	50.0	65.8	133.8	154.4

Source: Department of Health

To estimate the number of "occupied beds", information about occupancy rates is needed. The occupancy rates used here are those reported by the surveys by Laing and Buisson (the specialists in market research for private health, nursing and residential care) in June 1991, August 1992 and January 1994, which were 92 per cent, 94.6 per cent and 91.4 per cent respectively (Source: Laing and Saper (1999)). Because the change in the number of nursing home residents between 1991 and 1993 is very important for time path of the number of residents of communal establishments between 1991 and 1996, the method by which the number of "occupied beds" in nursing homes in 1991, 1992 and 1993 must be described. None of the three occupancy rates refers to the end of March. For 1991, 1992 and 1994 the time differences are small and the occupancy rates can be taken as applying to end March as well. But for end March 1993, a percentage is interpolated, pro rata to time, between August 1992 and January 1994. The beds are registered as being intended for the elderly, but not quite all are occupied by persons aged 65 and over. An adjustment for this is the other stage of working back from 1994. In Table E.2 the number of residents aged 65 and over at March 1994 sums to 132,400. From Table E.2 the number of registered beds times Laing and Buisson's occupancy rates gives 136,600 occupied beds in total. Taking both at face value implies 4,400 beds occupied by persons under 65, 3.2 per cent of all occupied beds.

Table E.3: Estimate of Nursing Home Residents Aged 65 and Over in 1991, 1992 and 1993				
	Registered beds (thousands) (A)	**Occupancy rate (per cent) (B)**	**Estimate of occupied beds (thousands) (C= A x B)**	**Residents aged 65+ (thousands = C - 3.2per cent)**
1991	109.0	92.0	100.3	97.1
1992	124.0	94.6	117.3	113.6
1993	144.3	93.3	134.6	130.3

For comparing the number of persons in the institutional population with the projection, the number of residents aged 75 and over in residential care homes and nursing homes is required. For residential care homes in all years from 1991 to 1996 and for nursing homes from 1994 onwards, residents aged 65-74 can be subtracted. For 1991, 1992 and 1993 an estimate has to be made for nursing home residents aged 65-74. The simplest method is pro rata to the total of residents aged 65 and over. Residents aged 65-74 are shown in Table E.2 as 14.4, 14.7, 13.9 and 13.5 per cent of all residents aged 65 and over in 1994, 1995, 1996 and 1997. These proportions are too low for small variations to make much difference to an estimate of the number of residents aged 75 and over. The proportion in 1994 is therefore assumed to have applied in 1991, 1992 and 1993 and hence the number of residents of nursing homes aged 65 - 74 are put at 14.0, 16.4 and 18.8 thousands respectively.

Change in the number of residents in residential care and nursing homes relative to population

The reported and estimated changes in the number of residents aged 75 and over in residential care homes and nursing homes has next to be compared with the change that there would be if ratios to population analysed by age range (75-79, 80-84 and 85 and over), sex and marital status remained unaltered from 1991. Information is not immediately available about residents of resident care homes and nursing homes in 1991 in this detail. But they are so high a proportion of all residents of communal establishments at ages 75 and over that a good approximation can be obtained by applying the 1991 ratios of all communal establishment residents to population to the official mid-year estimates of population by age, sex and marital status. Constant 1991 ratios to population is the assumption made for the 1992-based population projections of the institutional population. In Table E.4 these hypothetical figures are shown for comparison in index number form as they include residents of other types of communal establishment.

Table E.4:	Residents Aged 75 and Over in Residential Care and Nursing Homes Compared With Population				
	Residential care homes ('000)	Nursing homes ('000)	Total ('000)	Index (1991 = 100)	Change due to population (a) (Index 1991 = 100)
1991	207.6	83.0	291.0	100.0	100.0
1992	205.4	97.0	302.0	103.8	101.7
1993	202.8	112.0	315.0	108.2	103.3
1994	203.6	113.1	316.7	108.8	104.0
1995	203.8	115.6	319.4	109.8	106.2
1996	205.3	114.8	320.1	110.0	107.9

Note: (a) Includes changes in the proportions of males and females and in marital status

Men and women living in residential care homes and nursing homes are a very high proportion of the institutional population aged 75 and over, but not the totality. To assess how the institutional population as a whole has changed since 1991, allowance has to be made for residents in other categories of establishments, about 8.9 per cent of the institutional population aged 75 and over in 1991. For present purposes, a slow reduction should probably be assumed as a consequence of hospitals accommodating fewer long stay elderly patients. A reduction of 1 per cent per year is assumed for present purposes. On this assumption, the comparison of the estimated number of residents aged 75 and over in communal establishments with the hypothetical number that there would be if the ratio of residents in communal establishments to total population analysed by age (75-79, 80-84 and 85 and over), sex and legal marital status remained as in 1991 would be as in Table E.5. The indexes of residents of residential care homes and nursing homes and of the whole institutional population are shown to the first decimal place to avoid rounding errors.

Table E.5: Institutional Population 1991 to 1996 (Indexes 1991 = 100)			
	Residential care and nursing homes	Total Institutional Population	Hypothetical with constant ratios to total population
1991	100.0	100.0	100.0
1992	103.8	103.4	101.7
1993	108.2	107.3	103.3
1994	108.8	107.8	104.0
1995	109.8	108.6	106.2
1996	110.0	108.7	107.9

From the information about residents in residential care homes and nursing homes, the institutional population is estimated to have grown by about 4 per cent relative to population between 1991 and 1993. Between 1993 and 1996, however, there was an increase of only 1.3 per cent, as compared with the increase of 4.5 per cent that there would have been if ratios of institutional to total population had remained constant. These changes in the institutional population relative to what there would have been with constant ratios to total population can readily be explained. The number of residents in private nursing homes rose rapidly in the late 1980s and early 1990s, when the rules for payment of fees through Income Support made the number of residents virtually demand led. Very different arrangements were provided by the National Health Service and Community Care Act 1990, which came into effect at the beginning of April 1993. Access to public funding for care in residential or nursing homes was made conditional on a professional assessment by staff of local authority social services departments, which took account of the available alternatives and of limited budgets. This change of regime was expected to restrain the increase in the number of care residents and the run of figures in Tables E.4 and E.5 shows clearly that it did so.

Projections for post 1996

In Table E.5 the estimated institutional population aged 75 and over in 1996 is shown as about 0.7 per cent higher than it would have been with constant (1991) ratios of institutional population to total population specific for age, sex and legal marital status, that is 0.7 per cent higher than would be given by applying the assumptions for the 1992-based household projections to the 1996 mid-year population estimate analysed by marital status. The mid-1996 institutional population is estimated at 349,000 compared with the 346,500 that the 1992-based assumptions would give. Whether the difference was spread pro rata across all population categories cannot be ascertained from the information available. A pro rata assumption, that all the ratios of institutional population to total population were 0.7 per cent higher in 1996 than in 1991 has therefore to form the start line for 1996-based projections.

After 1993, the institutional population aged 75 and over rose slowly, but by much less than it would have done with constant ratios to population. In the aggregate, ratios of institutional population to total population were falling, which counts heavily against retaining the previous assumption of constant ratios. The question is how fast and for how long the ratios of institutional population to projected population should be assumed to fall. Between 1993 and 1996 the decline in those ratios shown in Table E.5 was about 3 per cent, 1 per cent a year. Such a decline could well continue for a time. The number of new entrants year by year has been restrained and many men and women who went into nursing homes at the end of the 1980s will have died before long. That would produce a more rapid decline in the institutional population relative to the total population than there would be in the longer term without changes in policy. Residential and domiciliary care for elderly people has been reviewed by the Royal Commission on Long Term Care With Respect to Old Age which reported in March 1999. The Commission recommended that a larger proportion of care than now should be provided in people's own homes.

The assumption made for the 1996-based household projections is that in that ratio of institutional population to total population will decline between 1996 and 2001 at the rate estimated for 1993 - 96, 1.0 per cent a year and then remain constant from 2001 to 2021. The projections of the institutional population produced by these assumptions are shown in Table E.6. The numbers with ratios of institutional population to total population constant at 1991 levels (as in the 1992-based projections) are shown for comparison.

Table E.6 Projections of the Institutional Population Aged 15 and Over (thousands)							
	1991	1996	2001	2006	2011	2016	2021
1996-based projection							
15 - 74	374.6	374.6	374.6	374.6	374.6	374.6	374.6
75 and over	321.2	349.0	341.9	344.0	347.7	353.7	375.3
Total aged 15 and over	**695.7**	**723.6**	**716.5**	**718.6**	**722.3**	**728.3**	**749.9**
With constant 1991 ratios to total population at age 75 and over							
15 - 74	374.6	374.6	374.6	374.6	374.6	374.6	374.6
75 and over	321.2	346.5	357.0	359.2	363.0	369.3	391.9
Total aged 15 and over	**695.7**	**721.1**	**731.5**	**733.8**	**737.6**	**743.9**	**766.5**
Difference (= effect of 1996 assumptions)	**0**	**+2.5**	**-15.0**	**-15.2**	**-15.3**	**-15.6**	**-16.6**

A lower figure for the institutional population means a correspondingly higher figure for the private household population and consequently, other things being equal, a larger number of households. In comparison with the assumptions made in the 1992-based household projections, the assumptions for the 1992-based household projections reduce the number of households in 1996 by between 1,000 and 2,000 and increase the number in 2021.

ANNEX F

Difference between the 1992-based and 1996-based household projections

Reasons why a new projection differs from the previously projection that it supersedes are always important. But a particular reason for the interest in the reason why the 1996-based projections differs from the 1992-based projections that it replaces is that it is lower. Each of the three previous projections (1985; 1989-and 1992-based) was substantially higher that the one before, as Table 22 shows. So the reasons why the 1996-based projection of households has come out lower, notwithstanding a larger increase in the projected adult population, warrant a fairly detailed explanation.

The analysis of reasons for the different between the two household projections is concentrated on the figures for 2016, the terminal year of the 1992-based projections. The space required to included earlier figures is the main reason; but since the projection of marital status and household representative rate incorporate time trends, little additional insight would be gained by looking in detail at intermediate years. The differences would generally affect the same groups in the same directions, but by proportionally smaller amounts.

As a first stage, an analysis of the components of difference between the 1992-based and 1996-based household projections was shown for the categories of type of household distinguished in Table 18. The components of difference are those shown for all household types together in Table F.1.

Table F.1 Components of Difference Between Projections of Households in 2016: Analysis by Type of Household (thousands)					
	1992 proj	Population	Marital status	Institutional population	Household rep rates	1996 proj
Married couple households	9,945	+84	-761	+1	-19	9,251
Cohabiting couple households	1,579	+18	+1062	-	+1	2,660
Lone parent households	1,257	+25	-8	-	+23	1,296
Other multi-person households	2,240	+24	-116	+1	+23	2,172
One person households	8,577	+8	-574	+15	-93	7,934
All households	23,598	+159	-397	+17	-65	23,313
Concealed couples	60	+1	+8	-	-2	67
Concealed lone parent families	83	-1	+5	-	+2	89

Married Couple and Cohabiting Couple Households

Only the population projections and the marital status projections contribute materially to the difference between the 1992-based and 1996-based projections of married and cohabiting couple households. The institutional population only affects the household projection at ages 75 and over. Household representative rates for married couples have been very high for many years except at the very youngest ages and cohabiting couples who live as members of someone else's household are very few. There is therefore very little scope for differences in projections of household representative rates. "Marital status" includes changes in the proportions cohabiting. The projected reduction in the married population (not quite the same as the married couple population owing to separated though legally married men and women) due to lower projected marriage rates and the increase in the cohabiting population owing to higher proportions of single men and women cohabiting are discussed in Annex D and need not be further discussed here. As would be expected, they predominate in explaining the change between the 1992-based and 1996-based projections of married couple and cohabiting couple households. The higher proportion of young single men and women cohabiting did not result in many fewer living as one-person households. As is shown in Table F.5, and effect it may have had, was more than offset by there being more single men and women in total due to lower marriage rates.

Lone parent households

The difference between the 1992-based and 1996-based projections of lone parent households is small. The increase due to higher household representative rates is mainly among legally never married women, some 17,000 out of the total 23,000 shown in Table F.1. Of 17,000, nearly 6,000 are at ages under 30 and the rest mainly aged 30-49. That is likely to reflect an increase in the number of lone mothers who are legally single, but who bore their children while cohabiting.

Other multi-person households

As it is shown in Tables 9 and 10, "other multi-person households" are a very diverse group. It is therefore to be expected that the components of difference between the 1992-based and 1996-based projections would impact in different ways on the sub categories of multi-person households. The effect of the higher population appears straightforward and too few of the "other multi-person households" have representatives aged 75 and over for the institutional population to have a significant effect. But there is considerable scope for the marital status and household representative rate differences to impact differently. First an analysis is made of the differences due to marital status and household representative rates according to sex and marital household representative.

Table F.2 Difference between Projections of Other Multi-Person Households in 2016: Analysis by Sex and Marital Status		
	Difference due to	
	Marital status	Household representative rates
Household representative: Male		
Never married	-3	-6
Divorced and separated	-50	+24
Widowed	-8	+2
Household representative: Female		
Never married	+24	-1
Divorced and separated	-20	-7
Widowed	-59	+11
Total	**-116**	**+23**

The differences due to marital status follow directly from the marital status projection (Tables D.9 and D.10). The differences due to household representative rates require a more detailed analysis. In Table F.3 the difference between the 1992-based and 1996-based projections of "other multi-person households" due to household representative rates are cross-analysed by age and marital status. All are non-cohabiting by definition.

Table F.3 Difference in Projections of Other Multi-Person Household in 2016 Due to Household Representative rates: Further Analysis (thousands)

	Age of representative				
	Under 30	30 - 44	45 - 64	65 & over	Total
Household representative: Male					
Never married	-9	-1	+3	-	-6
Divorced and separated	+1	+1	+5	+17	+24
Widowed	-	-	-2	+4	+2
Household representative: Female					
Never married	+3	-6	+2	-	-1
Divorced and separated	-	+1	+3	-12	-7
Widowed	-	-	-1	+11	+11
Total	**-5**	**-5**	**+10**	**+20**	**+23**

Changes to household representative rates for a particular type of household, in the instance, "other multi-person households" can be the consequence of a shift between types of household; e.g. more young single men living alone instead of in a multi-person household, or a change in the proportion that are household representatives overall. The effects of changing other multi-person household rates shown in Table F.3 have therefore to be looked at alongside the effect of different one person household representative rates (Table F.6).

One person households

Overall, the reduction in the number of one person households is the main explanation of the difference between the 1992-based and 1996-based projections. A detailed analysis is first made in the same terms as in Table F.1 for one person households classified by sex and marital status.

That overall difference between the projected number of one person households in 2016 due to population is only 8 thousand is explained by the reduction in the projection of the population aged 85 and over (see Annex C, Table C.10). This impacts primarily on the number of widows and widowers, though with smaller effects on the number of single and divorced men and women.

Table F.4 Components of the Difference Between projections of One Person Households in 2016 (thousands)

	1992 proj	Population	Marital status	Institutional population	Household rep rates	1996 proj
Household representative: Male						
Never married	2,355	+35	-61	+1	-23	2,307
Divorced and separated	1,376	+12	-150	-	-45	1,193
Widowed	540	-15	-19	+2	-4	503
Household representative: Female						
Never married	1,204	+17	+95	+1	+8	1,325
Divorced and separated	928	+3	-35	+1	-11	886
Widowed	2,174	-44	-403	+10	-17	1,719
Total	**8,577**	**+8**	**-573**	**+15**	**-93**	**7,634**

For marital status, a cross analysis by age is required, since the extent of the change between the projections differs with age. "Marital status" here includes the effect of increases in the proportion of never married men and women cohabiting being assumed in the 1996-based but not the 1992-based projections.

Table F.5	Difference in Projections of One Person Households in 2016 Due to Marital Status: Further Analysis (thousands)				
	Age of representative				
	Under 30	30 - 44	45 - 64	65 & over	Total
Household representative: Male					
Never married	+19	+18	-64	-34	-61
Divorced and separated	-23	-81	-25	-21	-150
Widowed	-	-	-9	-11	-19
Household representative: Female					
Never married	+62	+107	-56	-17	+95
Divorced and separated	-12	-17	+2	-9	-35
Widowed	-	-1	-75	-327	-403
Total	**+46**	**+26**	**-227**	**-419**	**-573**

In projections of households in 2016, the impact on the number of one person households of the assumption that the proportion of never married men who cohabit will rise is principally at ages 45 and over. As explained in Annex D, this part of the marital status projection assumes that cohabiters will continue in that status as they grow older, hence an increase with time in the cohabiting population in middle age and above. At the younger ages, the fall in marriage rates that is projected results in a large enough increase in the never married population for the increased proportion cohabiting not to produce an actual fall in the non-cohabiting population. The assumption that the population of never married men and women who cohabit will rise is thus more than offset in its effect on the projected number of young single men and women living as one person households by the lower marriage rates.

The lower projected number of divorced one person households is due mainly to the smaller divorced population that is projected, not to more cohabitation. As explained in Annex D, lower marriage rates reduce the population at risk to divorce, so with broadly constant age specific divorce rates, the projected divorce population is reduced. Among men this impacts primarily on one person households, among women it affects lone parent households.

The impact of the revised projection of the proportion of women who are widows (see also Annex D) is shown by comparison of Table F.2 and F.5 to be for the most part one person households. The resulting difference from this cause between the 1992-based and 1996-based projections is 403,000 one person households, 59,000 "other multi-person households" and 7,000 lone parent households with dependent children.

A similar analysis by age as well as marital status is also needed for the effect of difference between the 1992-based and 1996-based household representative rates. This is shown in Table F.6.

| Table F.6 | Difference in Projections of One Person Households in 2016 Due to Household Representative Rates: Further Analysis (thousands) | | | | |

	Age of representative				
	Under 30	30 - 44	45 - 64	65 & over	Total
Household representative: Male					
Never married	-5	-6	-8	-5	-23
Divorced and separated	+1	-6	-22	-18	-45
Widowed	-	-	-	-4	-4
Household representative: Female					
Never married	+23	-4	-3	-8	+8
Divorced and separated	-1	-3	+5	-13	-11
Widowed	-	-1	-	-17	-17
Total	**+18**	**-19**	**-28**	**-65**	**-93**

The effects of different household representative rates on the projected number of one person households was concentrated in the older age groups. The effect of the revised projections of household representative rates (the result of incorporation post 1992 information) on the projected number of young single men living as one person households is small. The new information has led to the projection of young single women being raised.

ANNEX G

Analyses of sensitivity of the household projections to changes in the underlying assumptions and to economic conditions

The House of Commons Select Committee on the Environment, Transport and the Regions recommended that with the next household projections the Government should publish an analysis which shows the effect of small changes in the assumptions underlying the projections. In its reply (CM 4080, October 1998), the Government stated that: "The Department... will publish suitable sensitivity analyses alongside the next set of household projections" (paragraph 125). This annex provides the detail of the sensitivity analyses presented in summary form in Table 16 and 17 of the commentary.

The sensitivity analyses presented fall into four groups:

(a)   Variant assumptions for the official population projections, i.e. about births, deaths and migration.

(b)   Variant assumptions for the official projections of marital status and cohabitation.

(c)   Variant projections of household representative rates.

(d)   Variant assumptions about key components of economic conditions, i.e the rate of rise of real income, unemployment rates and interest rates.

The variant assumptions about economic conditions are different in status from the other variants. Births, deaths, migration, marital status, cohabitation and household representative rates are the components of the population projections and the household projections derived from them. The household projections do not explicitly incorporate assumptions about the future course of the economy. Household representative rates are projected by time trends fitted to Census and Labour Force Survey data points (see Annex B), of which there are too few for estimating the effect of the economic variables, particularly as time lags may be present. The indicators of how sensitive the future increase in households might be to economic conditions were obtained from a different source, the model prepared for the Department of the Environment, Transport and the Regions by the Department of Applied Economics, Cambridge (DAE). The DAE model was prepared for estimating demand and need for social housing, in which future numbers of households is one of the intermediate stages.

Population projection variants

As part of the national population projections, the Government Actuary's Department (GAD) calculated variant projections with alternative assumptions about births, deaths and migration. These variant projections are described in Chapter 4 of *National population projections 1996-based, PP2 No 21*. These variants, as published, were calculated for the United Kingdom. For clarity about the link with the official demographic projections, the population differences are shown in this Annex in UK terms. The England and Wales equivalents were used to produce variant household projections which were then scaled (pro rata to population) to England so as to derive from them measures of the sensitivity of household projections for England to changes in the demographic assumptions. The variant assumptions about births, deaths and migration are summarised in Table G.1. The detail of the fertility and mortality assumptions is more complex than can be conveyed by figures in a table and is in Chapter 4 of *National population projections 1996-based*.

Table G.1: High, Low and Principal Projection Assumptions for the 1996-Based Population Projections	Low	Principal	High
Fertility			
Long term average number of children per woman	1.60	1.80	2.00
Mortality - increase in expectation of life at birth between 1996 and 2021 (years)			
Male	4.4	3.6	2.6
Female	3.7	3.1	2.4
Migration			
Net inward migration per year from 1998 - 99 onwards (thousand)	25	65	105

The effects of these alternative assumptions on the projected UK population, analysed by age, are shown in Table G.2. The tables show the population aged 20 and over: boys and girls under age 16 do not head households and household heads aged 16 - 19 are few.

Table G.2: Difference in Projected UK Population Resulting from High and Low Variant Assumptions (thousands)	2011		2021	
	High	**Low**	**High**	**Low**
Fertility				
20 - 29	nil	nil	+100	-166
Total aged 20 and over	**nil**	**nil**	**+100**	**-166**
Mortality				
20 - 59	-23	+12	-46	+22
60 - 74	-42	+32	-87	+71
75 - 84	-50	+43	-102	+88
85 and over	-52	+47	-105	+101
Total aged 20 and over	**-167**	**+134**	**-340**	**+282**
Migration				
20 - 29	+127	-127	+175	-175
30 - 39	+195	-195	+253	-253
40 - 49	+98	-98	+247	-247
50 - 59	+44	-44	+121	-121
60 and over	+31	-31	+81	-81
Total aged 20 and over	**+495**	**-495**	**+877**	**-877**

Source: *National population projections 1996-based*, Tables 4.2, 4.3 and 4.6

Marital status and cohabitation variants

Official projections of the legal marital status of the population (C Shaw, "1996-based population projections by legal marital status for England and Wales", *Population Trends No 95*, March 1999) and of the cohabiting population (C Shaw and J Haskey, "New estimates and projections of the population cohabiting in England and Wales", *Population Trends No 95*, March 1999) are for England and Wales. So too therefore are variant projections and differences from the principal projections.

Variant projections of the legal marital status of the population were made with (separately) higher and lower assumptions about marriage and divorce rates. The variant assumptions about marriage rates are that first marriage rates and remarriage rates will gradually diverge from the principal projection until 2011 when they will stabilise at 15 per cent higher or lower and 10 per cent higher and lower respectively. These assumptions are used to project the legal marital status of the population with divorce rates as in the principal projection. The higher and lower divorce rate variants assume that divorce rates will gradually diverge from the assumption used in the principal projection until 2011 and then stabilise at 10 per cent higher or lower than in the principal projection. The implications of these assumptions for the proportions of men and women ever marrying and the proportion of first marriages ending in divorce are shown in Table G.3.

Table G.3: Proportions of Men and Women Ever Marrying and of First Marriages Ending in Divorce (per cent)				
	1995 - 96		2011 - 12 onwards	
	Male	Female	Male	Female
Proportion ever married				
Principal assumption	67	73	66	71
High marriage rate	...	...	71	76
Low marriage rate	...	...	60	65
Proportion of first marriages ending in divorce				
Principal assumption	39	38	38	38
High divorce rate	...	...	41	41
Low divorce rate	...	...	35	35

Note: The rates shown are based on the rates for 1995 - 96 and 2011 - 12. See the note to Table D.2 about the proportions ever married and divorced.

Source: *1996-based projections of the population by legal marital status*, Table 3

Another way of depicting the variant marriage and divorce assumptions is the number of marriages and divorces they imply in selected years.

Table G.4 Number of Marriages and Divorces on Alternative Assumptions (thousands)				
	1996	2001	2011	2021
Marriages				
Principal assumption	279	274	296	303
High marriage rate	...	282	327	330
Low marriage rate	...	265	263	272
Divorces				
Principal assumption	157	141	118	109
High divorce rate	...	144	128	118
Low divorce rate	...	137	108	100

Source: As Table G.3

The differences made to the projected legal marital status of the population are shown in Table G.5. Since the total adult population is the same for all assumptions, the increases and decreases must sum to zero, apart from rounding. A given percentage difference in marriage rates has a much greater effect on projected marital status than the same percentage difference in divorce rates, because the number of marriages is much larger.

Alternative projections of cohabitation have also been published (Shaw and Haskey (1999) Table 4). The higher and lower variants start with 1996 base proportions cohabiting within each age/sex/legal marital status category, 2.5 per cent higher or lower than the principal projection, to reflect uncertainties about the base estimates. The variant projected paths then gradually diverge from the principal projection until 2011, when the proportion of never married men and women cohabiting is 20 per cent higher or lower and the proportion of divorced, separated and widowed men and women cohabiting 10 per cent higher or lower. Table G.6 shows the differences in the projected number of cohabiting couples, classified by the legal marital status of the male partner.

Table G.5: Projected Legal Marital Status: Differences from Principal Projection (thousands)

	Never married	Married	Widowed	Divorced
High marriage				
2001	-23	+29	-1	-5
2011	-333	+375	-4	-38
2021	-771	+807	-2	-33
Low marriage				
2001	+24	-29	-	+5
2011	+346	-389	+4	+39
2021	+837	-864	+1	+26
High divorce				
2001	-	-11	-	+12
2011	-	-123	-1	+124
2021	-	-234	-7	+241
Low divorce				
2001	-	+11	-	-11
2011	-1	+124	+2	-125
2021	-1	+240	+6	-245

Source: See Table G.3

Table G.6   Differences from Principal Projections of Cohabiting Couples (thousands)

	Male partner			
	Never married	Divorced	Separated or widowed	Total
High cohabitation				
1996	+25	+11	+2	+39
2001	+119	+25	+5	+148
2011	+413	+55	+8	+475
2021	+473	+52	+7	+533
Low cohabitation				
1996	-26	-11	-2	-39
2001	-119	-25	-4	-149
2011	-413	-55	-7	-475
2021	-474	-53	-7	-533

Source: Shaw and Haskey (1999), Table 4

By the end of the projection period (2021), the variant assumptions produced figures for cohabiting couples 18 per cent higher or lower than in the principal projection. These variant assumptions about cohabitation are applied to the principal projection of legal marital status, the projected number of legally married men and women and hence married couples is the same for each of the assumptions about cohabitation. More or less cohabitation is therefore not even partially offset by less or more marriage.

Demographic sensitivity analysis for the household projections

The spans between the principal and variant projections of fertility, mortality, migration, marriage rates, divorce rates and cohabitation are used here as bases for indicators of household projection sensitivities because they have an official provenance. The published variant projections of marital status and cohabitation (Tables G.3, G.4, G.5 and G.6) were for England and Wales. The household projections sensitivities calculated from these variant projections and shown in Table G.7 therefore refer strictly speaking to England and Wales. For the migration variant the effect for England would be the same as for England and Wales; for other variants between 5 and 6 per cent less. The variant assumptions are described in very summary form; the further descriptions are earlier in this Annex.

Table G.7: Change in Projected Net Increase in Households 1996 - 2021 In Response to long term Changes in Demographic Assumptions (thousands)	
Fertility	
+0.2 in mean number of children per woman	+40
-0.2 in mean number of children per woman	-60
Mortality	
Decrease between 1996 and 2021 (relative to the principal projections) in the expectation of life at birth 1.0 years for males, 0.7(*) years for females	-180
Additional increase between 1996 and 2021 in the expectation of life at birth 0.8 years for males, 0.6 years for females	+160
Migration	
Net inward migration 40,000 a year higher	+450
Net inward migration 40,000 a year lower	-410
Marriage	
First marriage rates 15 per cent higher, remarriage rates 10 per cent higher	-100
First marriage rates 15 per cent lower, remarriage rates 10 per cent lower	+110
Divorce	
Divorce rates 10 per cent higher	+60
Divorce rates 10 per cent lower	-60
Cohabitation	
Proportion of never married persons cohabiting 20 per cent higher, formerly married 10 per cent higher	-180
Proportion of never married persons cohabiting 20 per cent lower, formerly married 10 per cent lower	+180
Note: (*) Difference from Table G.1 due to rounding	

Household representative rate sensitivities

Sensitivities to small changes in either direction in projected household representative rates can be shown only where the rates given by the main projection are sufficiently below 100 per cent for higher as well as lower alternatives to be meaningful. 100 per cent is, by definition, the maximum value when all members of a group defined by age, sex, legal marital status and cohabitation are household representatives. That position was closely approached long ago by married men whose wives were with them. By the end of the projection period, the projections imply that the rates will be not far short of 100 per cent for widows and widowers not living in institutions and all but young non-cohabiting divorced men (and women). That leaves single (in the sense of never legally married) men and women. For cohabiting men, the household representative rates is almost 100 percent, for cohabiting women it is zero (by definition - see Annex A); so higher or lower values than the main projection must apply to non-cohabiting never married men and women. Their projected household representative rates between ages 20 and 64 are shown in Table G.8, with 1981 and 1991 for comparison. Household representative rates at ages 15-19 are not shown because they are liable to distortion through differences in the mix of individual ages. At ages above 65, the numbers of single men and women are small.

Table G.8: 1996-Based Projected Household Representative Rates for Non-Cohabiting Never Married Men and Women (per cent)					
	1981	1991	1996	2011	2021
Men					
20 - 24	9.1	12.9	15.3	19.4	21.1
25 - 29	26.4	37.2	41.1	49.6	52.2
30 - 34	35.7	50.9	56.4	68.6	72.4
35 - 39	38.3	53.2	60.3	74.4	79.1
40 - 44	41.2	52.7	58.8	72.5	78.2
45 - 49	46.2	55.6	60.1	70.6	75.8
50 - 54	56.3	62.4	64.9	71.9	75.6
55 - 59	67.8	72.6	73.9	78.5	80.9
60 - 64	76.5	81.8	82.6	86.6	88.4
Women					
20 - 24	12.2	18.0	21.4	24.8	26.0
25 - 29	32.2	43.6	51.4	59.7	62.0
30 - 34	44.4	58.7	68.2	76.4	78.4
35 - 39	46.9	62.5	71.9	80.9	82.9
40 - 44	46.0	60.5	68.9	79.8	82.6
45 - 49	46.9	58.6	65.0	76.1	80.1
50 - 54	51.7	60.3	64.9	74.0	78.1
55 - 59	59.0	64.7	69.0	75.8	78.8
60 - 64	65.6	70.8	73.8	78.6	80.6

At the younger ages, female household representative rates are raised relative to male by lone parenthood. But both for men and women, household representative rates rose strongly between 1981 and 1996, with further rises projected in the quarter century to 2021. To show the effect of a small change in assumptions about household representative rates, a calculation is made of the effect of changing the projected rate for non-cohabiting never married men and women by one half of a percentage point, plus or minus, per five year period, that is to say by $1\frac{1}{2}$ percentage points by 2011 and $2\frac{1}{2}$ percentage points by 2021. The result of varying the projected increase in household representative rates in this way would be to raise or lower the projected number of households by **114,000** in 2011 and **201,000** in 2021. The effect of changing the projected household representative rates is linear: the difference made by varying the rates by 2 percentage points (e.g. from 50 to either 48 or 52) is twice as great as the difference made by 1 percentage point.

Sensitivity of future increases in the number of households to economic conditions

The official 1996-based household projections, like all their predecessors, do not embody explicit assumptions about economic conditions during the projection period. The projections are derived from projections of the private household population and marital status by applying household membership rates that are themselves projected by means of trends fitted to past values. The data points are the 1971, 1981 and 1991 Censuses and the Labour Force Survey from 1983 to 1997. These data points for household membership rates are too few, given sampling variability in the Labour Force Survey, and the likelihood of time lags, to model household representative rates as a function of economic variables such as real income, real interest rates and unemployment, together with non economic variables. Nevertheless, it is plausible to envisage the future increase in the number of households being greater if economic conditions are generally benign with rising real income, low real interest rates and low unemployment than if conditions are adverse with slow growth, high real interest rates and persistent unemployment. For example, rising real incomes influence the number of people that can afford to live independently.

Economic conditions could perhaps affect marital status, household representative rates, fertility and mortality rates, divorce and marriage rates and migration. The least difficult to model are the impacts on household representative rates. This is important, because of the total projected increase in households in 1996 - 2021, household representative rates explain only 24 per cent (Table 4 of the report). Moreover, part of the increase in household representative rates, particularly at the higher ages, is due to cohort effects unlikely to be influenced by economic conditions.

The growth rate in households are modelled as functions of economic variables in the model of demand and need for social housing prepared by the Department of Applied Economics, Cambridge (DAE) for the DETR. The basic structure of the model, though not the most recent work on it, was published by DETR, *An Economic Model of Demand and Need for Social Housing* (November 1997). The model was not set up specifically to produce household projections or forecasts, which are an intermediate product. Owing to the size of the sample available in the source used (the General Household Survey), equations for household growth could be estimated for only three age groups: 15-29, 30-59 and 60 and over. Equations were estimated for headship rates for each of the three groups, with real income (represented by consumers' expenditure), unemployment and real interest rates among the explanatory variables. The model could then be used along with assumed future values for the economic variables to make conditional forecasts of growth in the total numbers of households up to 2021.

Following this procedure with alternative values for the economic variables provides a way of estimating the sensitivity of the future increase in the number of households (within the DAE model) to differences in the rate of rise of real income, the level of unemployment and real interest rates. These would appear to be the economic variables that could affect household formation through readily visible routes. All the assumptions related to medium term trend values. The differences in value of economic variables taken for calculating sensitivities of the net increase in households are:

Real income (represented by real consumers' expenditure in the model): plus or minus 0.25 per cent a year.

Unemployment: plus or minus 1 percentage points.

Real interest rates: plus or minus 1 percentage points.

The differences made to the projected number of households in 2021 are shown in Table G.9. These changes vary slightly according to the direction of change in each economic factor because there are non-linear relationships in many key equations in the DAE model.

Table G.9 Sensitivities of Future Household Numbers in 2021 to Economic Assumptions (DAE Model) (thousands)	
Real gross domestic product (GDP) per head	
+0.25 per cent a year	+190
-0.25 per cent a year	-150
Real interest rates	
1 percentage point higher	-230
1 percentage point lower	+260
Unemployment	
1 percentage point higher	-20
1 percentage point lower	+30

ANNEX H

The Household Projection Service

Household projections for counties in a format similar to that for Government Office Regions are being sent to all strategic planning authorities to be used as background information for the regional planning process. These are available on request from:

Housing Data and Statistics
DETR
1/H3
Eland House
Bressenden place
London SW1E 5DU

A household projection service is available from the Population and Housing Research Group at Anglia Polytechnic University. This will make available more detailed information from the household projection data with the usual caveat that projections are less reliable the greater the degree of geographical dissaggregation and the further into the future they are taken. The household projection service will also undertake specific commissions using DETR's household projection methodology, for example to make projections based on customers own data.

All enquiries regarding provision and cost of the service should be made to:

Household Projection Service
PHRG
Anglia Polytechnic University
Victoria Road South
Chelmsford
Essex CM1 1LL

or telephone: 01245 357870
     fax   01245 493136

ANNEX I

Bibliography and references

Allnutt D E, Cox R T and Mullock P J. 'The projections of households', *Statistics for Town and County Planning*, Series III, Number 1, 1970

Corner I E. *A technical summary of the DOE household projection method*, Building Research Establishment Note, N57/92, 1992

DAE, *An Economic Model of Demand and Need for Social Housing*, DETR, 1997

DoE, 'Housing Policy: Technical Volume to Cmnd 6851, Part I', HMSO, 1977

DoE, *1981-based Estimates of Numbers of Households*, DoE 1985

DoE, *1983-based Estimates of Numbers of Households*, DoE 1986

DoE, *1985-based Estimates of Numbers of Households*, DoE 1989

DoE, *Household projections England 1989-2011*, HMSO 1991

DoE, *Projections of Households in England to 2016*, HMSO 1995

DETR, *Planning for Communities of the Future*, Cm 3885, February 1998

DETR, *Reply to the House of Commons Environment Committee Inquiry 1998*, Cm 4080, May 1998

Haskey J, 'Estimated numbers of one parent families and their dependent children', *Population Trends* No. 94, Winter 1998

Laing W. and Saper P., 'Promoting the development of a flourishing independent sector alongside good quality public services', Table 1 in *Royal Commission on Long Term Care, With Respect to Old Age*, Research volume 3, Cm 4192 - II/3, 1999

Morris, M, 'The rebased 1991 population estimates by marital status', *Population Trends* 88, Summer 1997

ONS, *International Migration*, ONS Series MN No 19, HMSO, 1994

ONS, *International Migration*, ONS Series MN No 20, HMSO, 1995

ONS, *International Migration*, ONS Series MN No 21, HMSO, 1996

ONS, *International Migration*, ONS Series MN No 22, TSO, 1997

ONS, *International Migration*, ONS Series MN No 23, TSO, 1998

ONS, *Subnational population projections for England 1996-based*, ONS Series PP3 no 10, 1999

ONS and DETR, *Housing in England 1995/96*, TSO, 1997

ONS and DETR, *Housing in England 1996/97*, TSO, 1998

ONS and DETR, *Housing in England 1997/98*, TSO, 1999

ONS and GAD, *National Population Projections: 1996-based*. ONS Series PP2 No 21. TSO, 1999

OPCS Occasional Paper No 42, National population projections; a new methodology for determining migration assumptions, a report by the Government Actuary's Department, HMSO, 1993

Shaw, C. '1996-based national population projections', *Population Trends*, 91, Spring 1998

Shaw, C. '1996-based population projections by legal marital status for England and Wales', *Population Trends*, 95, Spring 1999

Shaw, C and Haskey J. 'New estimates and projections of the population cohabiting in England and Wales', *Population Trends*, 95, Spring 1999

Vickers, L. 'Trends in migration in the UK', *Population Trends*, 94, Winter 1998

Wood, J., Horsfield, G. and Vickers, L. 'New subnational population model: methodology and uses' Population Trends, forthcoming 1999.

Statistical Publications from the Department of the Environment, Transport and the Regions

The Stationery Office Publications

Housing and Construction Statistics - Annual

Most of the tables in this reference book on housing and construction topics show how things have changed over the last eleven years; others give detailed analyses for the latest year. The quantity and type of housing built each year and the size of stock, improvements and energy conservation, slum clearance, rents and rent rebates, house prices and mortgage payments can all be derived from this publication. It also contains figures on the volume and type of construction work and new orders in Great Britain, the labour market, costs and prices of materials and labour, and the use of materials. Detailed analyses of the activities of private contractors and local authorities direct labour departments are given for recent years.

Housing and Construction Statistics - Quarterly

Produced in two parts each quarter designed to supplement the annual volume by making the latest figures available as quickly as possible.

Local Housing Statistics - Quarterly

This publication gives regular statistics on the progress of housebuilding, house renovations, council house sales and action in respect of homeless households in individual local authorities in England and Wales. Statistics on slum clearance and homes specially designed for elderly and the chronically sick and disabled are included as they become available.

Housing in England 1997/98

This report presents a comprehensive picture of housing in England, including:

Trends in tenure and the changing demographic and economic profiles of owners, social renters and private renters

Peoples's views about their accommodation and the area in which they live

The report also presents the latest information about privately renting tenancy groups, the housing costs and financial circumstances of owners and renters, waiting lists for council housing and movements between tenures.

Digest of Environmental Statistics - Annual

This Digest provides information on the main trends in environmental protection. Its explanatory text and commentary highlights the trends, gives information on some of the factors likely to influence them and, where appropriate, links series together. It has sections on global atmosphere, air quality, inland water, marine waters, radioactivity, noise, waste and recycling, land cover and use and wild life. A separate section updates the series on water supply and use.

Local Government Financial Statistics - Annual

This publication presents details of local authority expenditure and income during the last financial year. The main figures relate to local authorities in England, but summary figures are also shown separately for the various types of authority (counties and districts, metropolitan and non-metropolitan) in both England and Wales. Further tables set the total of local authority expenditure in the context of the whole of the national economy, and relate present levels of expenditure with those recorded in earlier years.

The Stationery Office publications are available from their bookshops at the addresses given on the back cover.

Department of the Environment, Transport and the Region Publications

Land Use Change in England

This bulletin presents the results of the Department's statistics on changes in land use, based on data recorded by Ordnance Survey as part of its work on map revision.

Development Control Statistics

This annual publication provides details of planning statistics handled by local planning authorities in England. It also contains information on planning appeals and data on land with outstanding planning permission for private housing development.

The above publications are available from the:

The Department of the Environment, Transport and the Regions Publications Sales Centre Unit 21, Goldthorpe Industrial Estate Goldthorpe Rotherham S63 9BL

☎ *01709 - 891318*